Changing Times
SERIES

The Meadows
remembered

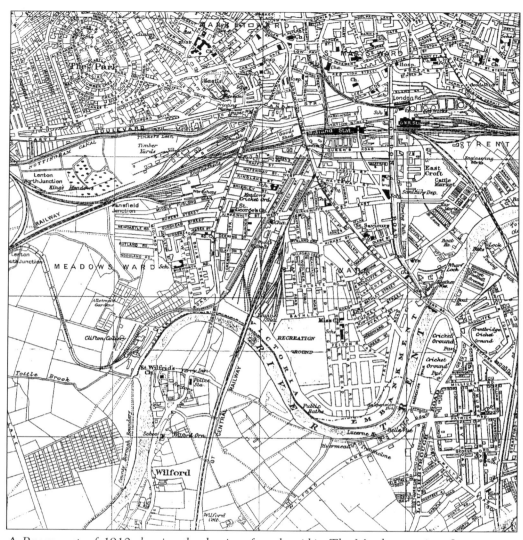

A Bacon map of 1910 showing the density of roads within The Meadows region. Its east-west boundaries are marked roughly by London Road and the cattle market (near the top right) stretching across towards, bottom left, the recently-sunk mine shafts of Clifton Colliery. The north-south perimeters are marked by the Midland Station and its railway line travelling east and the River Trent's undulating course around Wilford and the Trent Embankment. Note the cluttered streets of St Mary's Ward near Hollow Stone and the Lace Market in the extreme top right and the Great Central Railway line that cuts a swathe through the very heart of The Meadows, almost parallel to the grandiose tree-laden Queen's Walk. Although the Forest football ground and the Trent Bridge cricket ground are established to the south-east of the Trent, there is as yet no sign of Meadow Lane. The ground, destined to be the home of Notts County, was under construction in the summer of 1910 and was opened officially on 3 September of that year. (map reproduced by courtesy of Nottinghamshire Archive Office)

Changing Times
SERIES

The Meadows
remembered

David McVay

TEMPUS

First published 2000
Reprinted 2004
Copyright © David McVay, 2000

Tempus Publishing Limited
The Mill, Brimscombe Port,
Stroud, Gloucestershire, GL5 2QG

ISBN 0 7524 1890 4

Typesetting and origination by
Tempus Publishing Limited
Printed in Great Britain

Cover picture: *Floodwaters on Middle Furlong Road in March 1947 from the pages of the* Nottingham Evening News (*now the* Nottingham Evening Post).

Eva Trueman's old house on the original Kirkewhite Street. She was one of the last out when the houses were demolished in 1943.

Contents

Left: *The way they were: Vera Stafford and her neighbour Mrs Heathcoat clean up in King's Meadow Road.* Right: *Jean Taylor's mother on her doorstep.*

Foreword

For Richer, for Poorer

Poor but happy. If there is a recurring theme in this people's history of The Meadows district of Nottingham, it is that often expressed sentiment. One that is so open to ridicule amongst today's more affluent generation, a state that was mocked definitively in the *Monty Python* sketch that opined that the pinnacle of luxury and decadence was afforded by a childhood spent residing in a shoe box in the fast lane of the motorway as one of countless siblings.

True, the high density housing built on land adjacent to the north of the River Trent offered little respite to residents from the daily grind of work, rest and, for adults at least, a restricted amount of play that was the norm during the early to middle decades of the twentieth century.

And yet the impression created by the vast majority of correspondents who contributed to this book, and originally to the letters page and *Bygones* publication of the *Nottingham Evening Post*, is that life was anything but grinding drudgery in The Meadows.

Perhaps in a more genteel age of innocence, the simple things, the basic requirements and bare necessities sufficed. The pleasures of the Fifth of November, a stroll along the Victoria Embankment or a steamboat ride to Colwick Pleasure Park. Certainly those who experienced their coming of age there recall the classic street games, the wastelands and ruins where the imagination ran riot or swimming in a river still to be ravaged by the effects of pollution.

Of course there is the inevitable element of rose-tinted spectacles that focus attention when nostalgia and the past are topics of conversation. Maybe Arkwright Street, Wilford Road, the Leeny Gang and Mundella School were not quite the inspiring institutions former residents would have us believe. Geoffrey Oldfield, who puts the region in its historical context on the following pages, confirmed that many of the terraced and back to back housing was beyond redemption, its cramped walls rotten with damp and offering appalling sanitation. It was far from unusual to find lavatories confined to outside status with several families having to share the facility in a communal backyard.

Nevertheless, for the likes of Geoff Cowlishaw, it was a place where he lived, breathed and was catered for from the cradle to the grave. Born in 1929 at No. 47 Mundella Street he remained there until his death shortly before Christmas 1999. Like many 'Meadows born and bred folk' he was proud of his roots and took a keen interest in local events. In his letter and photograph, which are published on later pages in this book, he remembers the floods of 1947 that engulfed the landscape as water levels from the previously frozen Trent rose alarmingly in March of that year. If it was much to the dismay of adults, it came as a great joy to many children marooned from school but experiencing the inherent childhood joys of splashing about and getting a thorough soaking.

It is for such as Geoff and an entire generation of young and old Meadows people that this book should bear testament to their recollections of an irretrievable bygone age and region.

During the Corporation's slum clearance programme of the 1970s, bulldozers cut huge swathes through The Meadows, as its indigenous population was redistributed hastily to relatively distant and, more often than not, soulless locations. When the dust had settled, a unique community and its spirit had been demolished along with the bricks and mortar.

From the ashes, the new Meadows has arisen in a similar fashion to the St Ann's district of Nottingham which suffered the same fate in a decade of social reform that tended to err to the over-zealous. In more troubled times there is speculation that much of the latter's accommodation may be flattened to herald yet another fresh dawn.

Digital, mobile but often remote in attitude and control of their children may well be the characteristics attributed to the people of this millennium generation. Poor or happy they clearly are not.

David McVay

Childhood fantasies lived out in backyards between the terraced housing.

Acknowledgements

Michael Gardner, Douglas Whitworth, Harold Mercer, Geoffrey Oldfield, Diana Rees, Elena Hayward, the *Nottingham Evening Post* and *Bygones*, Jan Eastgate, Brian Watson, Vera Stafford, Harold and Mary Mettham, Ivy Clarkestone-Priestley, Jean Taylor, Sheila Manners, Joy Robinson-Judd, and far too many others to mention individually whose generosity and kindness merely epitomizes The Meadows spirit. My eternal gratitude.

For my wife Debby, for her tolerance, support and proof-reading; Tom, for his wit, wisdom and inspirational dexterity on the Play Station; and Jess for her smile, humour and for not spilling a single drop of Ribena on any of the photographs or manuscripts. My eternal love.

The construction of houses in Turney Street, 1902. Seen from the Trent Bridge tram shed, the men on the Corporation tower wagon are, from left to right: T. Houghton, H. Madden and the driver S. Simpson. Standing are foreman J. Burnt, wearing a bowler hat, Percy Abbott and B. Samons. (photograph: Jan Eastgate)

Introduction

In this definitive account of the region, local historian Geoffrey Oldfield offers an historical perspective on the region

The Meadows, Rise and Fall

Just after the Second World War, most people seem to have listened to a radio programme broadcast every Sunday morning at twelve noon. It was called *Two Way Family Favourites* and was a record request programme, designed to link troops in Germany in the British Army Occupation Rhine Force. It was presented by Cliff Michelmore in Germany and Jean Metcalf in London. One Sunday, Jean had a request from a family in Nottingham and she said the address conjured up a delightful picture. It was Crocus Street, The Meadows. It was, as residents knew, not quite the idyllic scene she had imagined.

Ninety years earlier, Thomas Hammond and Samuel Oscroft were able to produce pictures that showed crocuses in bloom in The Meadows, which was still not built upon. When the Anglo-

The Enclosure Act of 1845 was well intended but it was impotent in terms of enforcing the correct building regulations, an absence of which eventually resulted in the floods of 1932 and 1947 because of that earlier negligence. This is part of the Victoria Embankment in March 1947. (photograph: Brian Watson)

Saxons founded a settlement, which became the original town of Nottingham, they wisely chose the site on a high cliff, overlooking the Trent Valley. This site, today forming the Lace Market, had several advantages. It was easy to defend against hostile tribes and the land below, reaching the River Trent a mile away, was available for growing food crops. When the river overflowed in wet winters, the floods would leave silt behind when the Trent resumed its normal course, which was good for the crops. It also meant their homes high up on the cliff would not be flooded. This was something the town council in the mid-nineteenth century seemed to have overlooked when they started to build on The Meadows, as they had been called for centuries.

No building had taken place in the previous centuries because The Meadows, like the Sand Field and the Clay Fields, had been lands which the burgesses of the town had used as common agricultural areas in which they had valuable rights. They were opposed to any other development because of those rights, despite the need for the town to build on them, because of the increasing population.

From about 1750, when the population was around 10,000, the numbers of people kept increasing: 30,000 in 1801 and 50,000 by 1841. This had resulted in the old town becoming an over-crowded industrial one, instead of the pleasant appearance of earlier years. Visitors in the eighteenth century often commented on the elegant buildings with gardens and orchards.

In the 1840s, government inquiries into the health of towns described Nottingham as one of the worst in England for slums, in narrow courts and alleys, with only rudimentary facilities and sanitation. Because of this, the Corporation at last was able to buy off the burgesses by compensating them with payments for their loss of grazing rights. To this they obtained, in 1845, an Act of Parliament called the Enclosure Act. This was a well-intentioned Act, which sought to regulate building on the newly available lands. It prescribed proper standards for the houses to be built, which would have led to the creation of pleasant suburbs. Unfortunately, once building started, it was found that there were no real powers to enforce these conditions in The Meadows, particularly where each action was later to result in extensive flooding. In the twentieth century, in 1932 and again in 1947, the residents of The Meadows paid the price caused by the negligence of the early years.

There was one feature of this Enclosure Act which was to benefit Nottingham and still does. This was a requirement that some open spaces were to be left and that is why today we have the Arboretum, the Forest, Robin Hood Chase and (in The Meadows) a cricket ground, now a park, adjoining Kirkewhite Street and the tree-lined Queen's Walk.

No building took place on most of the land on the north bank of the Trent because it was outside the borough boundary and part of Wilford parish.

Salmon's map of Nottingham, published in 1861, shows the extent to which The Meadows had developed by then. The main street pattern had already been carried out, with Arkwright Street becoming the main approach to the centre of the town from Trent Bridge. Before this the approach to the town was along what was quite rightly then known as the Flood Road, later London Road. This was a most inconvenient entrance to the town via the steep Hollowstone. There were not many houses built at that time, building took place mainly on Derwent Street, Bruce Grove, Williersley Street and a block fronting on Arkwright Street, at the corner of Kirkewhite Street, extending back to Healey Street. An early necessity was in this block, the Sir Richard Arkwright public house. There were also a few buildings nearer to London Road mainly houses including Burton's Almshouses, but even here, despite the few houses there was another public house, the Greyhound. No doubt the landlord expected some trade from travellers into the town who had to pay tolls at the nearby toll-bar although this custom was about to be discontinued.

A little later, when Clifton Colliery was opened in 1870, houses were built nearby in what was to become the Bosworth Road area. This was still part of Wilford parish, and only became part of the borough when the boundaries were extended in 1877.

By 1881, the whole of Arkwright Street – as far as Ryehill Street on the east side and Bathley Street on the west – was built upon, mainly with shops and several more public houses, such as the Brown, the Meadows Inn and the New Bridge Inn, with the Queen's Hotel occupying a strategic position near the Midland Railway Station. Kirkewhite Streets East and West ran from London Road to Wilford Road and, like Arkwright Street, were mainly of shops and public houses. St Saviour's church had been built in 1863 and had its school attached, and the Wesleyan chapel on Kirkewhite Street also had a school. The Congregational church and the Police Lodge were at the corner of Queen's Walk and Kirkewhite Street.

Behind Arkwright Street and Kirkewhite Street was the grid pattern of residential streets, many of them such as Bunbury Street and Crocus Street having terraces of small houses. Many of the people who lived in The Meadows' houses chose to do so because it was near to their workplace which was important in the days before cheap transport. These places of work, usually close to the houses, included in 1881: F.F. & A. Cleaver (bleachers, dyers and lace

Above: *Briar Street survived the floods of 1947 but not the slum clearance programme of 1975.*
Below: *Briar Street, c. 1970. (photograph: Michael Gardner)*

dressers), Moses Mellor and family (hosiery machine makers and iron and brass founders), Foster & Cooper (steam cabinet works) and Blackburn & Houldgate (lace manufacturers). There were also many smaller workshops and the fact that all these used coal, as did all the houses, meant that the air was far less pure than it is today, although there were no exhaust fumes from vehicles. The Trent Bridge line of horse tramways provided a ten-minute service from 8.45 a.m. to 10.25 p.m. The horses, together with those pulling all kinds of delivery vehicles, did pollute the atmosphere to some extent, although this proved beneficial to the fortunate few who had gardens.

Two developments towards the end of the nineteenth century and beginning of the twentieth century extended the build up of The Meadows. The Great Central Railway from Victoria Station crossed Station Street, Queen's Road and Arkwright Street. It then crossed The Meadows on embankments with bridges, so there were no level-crossings, with a goods yard alongside Queen's Walk before crossing the River Trent on a handsome bridge, demolished a few years ago. The railway company built a number of houses near the line, mainly for its employees. Some of these, on Blackstone Street and Cromford Street, had bedrooms from which the occupants could almost shake hands with engine drivers. Another smaller group of houses which still survives was built along Glapton Road, with terraces named in alphabetical order, from Attercliffe to Ferriby, after places on the Great Central's line.

The south-east part of The Meadows was completed about this time when the former waterworks buildings were demolished allowing development of new houses and streets such as Pyatt Street and Woodward Street. This also allowed the fine riverside Victoria Embankment to be built and the lands as far as Queen's Walk were retained as open spaces. The Meadows' inhabitants were thus more fortunate in having such a 'lung' on their doorsteps compared to other industrial parts such as St Ann's.

A school board had been formed in 1870 to provide elementary schools when education became more or less compulsory. Queen's Walk School was opened in 1880, followed by similar schools in London Road and Bosworth Road. A major development was the building of Mundella Secondary School over one hundred years ago, followed by buildings nearby which became Collygate Road and Trent Bridge schools.

When electric tramways were introduced in 1901 The Meadows provided the first depot between Pyatt Street and Bathley Street.

Public swimming and private baths were built a little later on Muskham Street with a wash-house when the tramways stables were no longer needed. Most of the houses in this part of The Meadows were of better construction and are still there today. This was due to the fact that from 1874 all new buildings in Nottingham had to be built according to specifications and plans approved by the town council.

Cultural improvements took a little longer to arrive. By 1914 the area had two cinematograph houses, the Globe and the Midland Picture Palace, later the Queen's Cinema. When the talkies arrived, the Imperial on Wilford Road and the Grove on Mayfield Grove meant that there was a choice of five cinemas in The Meadows if the Plaza is considered to be there (although on the other side of Trent Bridge, up to 1951 it was still in the city). The rather handsome building on Wilford Grove was opened as a library in the 1920s and the Memorial Gardens and War Memorial were created at that time.

Sport was well catered for with Notts County's ground on Meadow Lane, and Nottingham Forest's on Trent side which, like the Plaza, was still in the city having earlier started out on the waterworks land. Rowing was popular, with clubs and clubhouses as well as boats which could be hired by the hour; paddle-steamers, and later motor boats, provided trips to Wilford or Colwick; whilst tennis and cricket were available on the Embankment. Angling was also well catered for with fishing-tackle shops selling bait, while the Trent was still clean and safe enough for swimming – the Corporation even providing rudimentary changing accommodation. Swimming races were held between the Suspension Bridge, built in 1908, and Trent Bridge.

One hundred years after the first houses were built in The Meadows, came the decision to start demolishing the worst ones. These had never been well built in many cases and were beyond repair, as well as being too small and crowded together to be improved. Other buildings were also cleared so that a comprehensive redevelopment scheme could take place.

The main elements in the new Meadows were the disappearance of the two through roads Arkwright Street and Wilford Road. This was done to divert the main flow of traffic from the residential areas. These two were planned in a different way, with the old street patterns changed with walks, closes and gardens, many of them retaining the old street names. Far fewer new houses were built than were demolished and The Meadows was spared the high-rise blocks of other redeveloped areas. Industry was relocated so that it did not clash with housing and new developments such as a day centre, health centre and bus routes through The Meadows were introduced.

Two churches, St Saviour's and St George's, were retained but the newer St Faith's is now a school. Mundella School has been demolished and Mundella Court, new houses and flats, built on its site. The older schools have gone and been replaced by modern single-storey buildings.

The goodbye kids of Rupert Street with demolition imminent. (photograph: Michael Gardner)

CHAPTER 1

Childhood

Jean Taylor (far left with bows in her hair, holding her sister Elaine) and Meadows children pictured on Talbot Street. Jean's other sister Sue is holding the baby.

Scholastic Assistance

I was very interested in various articles about Mundella School. My mother was a pupil there before the First World War and I too followed in her footsteps in 1927 after gaining what was called an 'assisted scholarship'. That meant that as my father was a butcher (Woolmer Road) he could afford to pay half the fees. I left in 1932 after gaining a matriculation exemption. My first master was a Mr Holbrook, then T.C. Thorpe (Timothy Titus), Tripe Jackson, Squeak Broadburn with Sammy Clarke (music). Lizzie Howell (history), Fanny May Moseley (English), Tommy Hilton (French). The headmaster was 'Gaffer' Wight (often in his cups).

R. Savidge

A Pocket Full of Memories

I wonder if anyone remembers the St John's Church School which was situated at the bottom of Station Street and London Road? It belonged to St George's church in The Meadows. It was a lovely building and downstairs was a very large room that contained two large snooker tables. It was sold to Boots in 1935. My father was the caretaker there for many years before moving to Queen's Walk School to be a caretaker there and finally to St Ann's Board School.

Mrs Sunderland (née Carnelly)

Maureen Ellingworth (left) with Valerie Kirk, Josephine and Maureen Coddington and little June Ellingworth.

An Imperial Rush

No. 1 Ebenezer Terrace, Clayton Street, off Queen's Drive was the house into which I was born in 1942. The houses were all close, we backed onto Winfield's coal merchant. Their son, Derek, used to play with my sister Doris. The communal yard was our playground. Errand running was our favourite chore whether it was Neale's the beer-off or England's the papershop or Blackcat's on Deering Street.

We were given money wrapped in a note from Mam for the shop which might be Meadow Dairy, Marsden's, Co-op or Dolly Blue, the hardware shop. Summer holidays from school were heaven. Our holidays consisted of going to Trent Bridge, the Ha'penny Bridge or the Memorial Gardens. I also remember the large houses on Queen's Drive and we wished we lived there passing them on the way to school.

Saturday was the fourpenny rush at the Imperial, then afterwards home to fetch a jug of ale from Neale's. Sunday to the Queen's Walk Congregational church so Mam and my stepdad can have a kip!

We moved to Clifton when I was eleven, but I married at seventeen and my husband and I moved back to Ryehill Cottages, Kirkewhite Street when I was nineteen. I had three children in this house but that's another Meadows story, still as memorable as when I was younger. Oh! What lovely days, even though we were bombed, then flooded.

Maureen Bevis (née Ellingworth)

A Thirst for the Past

My memories of The Meadows, were in the late 1950s. The reason for this is that my

Queen's Walk School in the early 1950s; Maureen Ellingworth is far left on the front row.

cousin Maureen and her husband Aubrey invited me to go and stay with them and their baby daughter Kim. Aubrey was a decorator and he had just finished the house on Rupert Street. It was so nice.

On the days I stayed, we went to all the shops on Arkwright Street window shopping of course and there were quite a few houses with the front rooms made into a shop. We went to the paddling pool at Trent Bridge and more cousins joined us to have fun, just like they still do today, along with the park at the side and all for free.

Last year my uncle came from Canada. We wandered up and down The Meadows in and out of the side-streets. 'Where's all the children gone, the marbles, skipping and the noise?' he asked. 'It's not like The Meadows I knew.' I said to him let's pretend we haven't been, some memories are best as they were. As we walked back over Trent Bridge way, Canadian geese were everywhere. I thought to myself they seemed to like it here – it's only Ray that was disappointed. It was the old Meadows that played an important part in his growing up years. He went to High School, played the piano, and cricket (he wasn't a kid that got dirty), but he was proud to be a Meadows boy. Maybe it was just the pubs he missed!

Jean Taylor

The old Imperial on Wilford Road as seen from Middle Furlong Road. It had become office premises by May 1976. (photograph: H.L. Mercer)

Grammar Grows in a Garden Shed!

Because my father worked for the LNER all his life I was born on the lower end of Bathley Street in the railway houses. We moved but not for long, and returned to live on Radcliffe Street, where I spent the next twenty years before getting married and moving to Canada.

I attended Collygate School, later moving to Trent Bridge Junior and Senior schools, whilst my sister attended Mundella. What fun us kids had in those days before television, we played street games and tied doorknobs together before knocking. During the war it was decided to split the classes up at school just in case. It didn't last long, but I remember about ten of us had

classes in a factory plant on Meadow Lane, just past the dairy. Classes also took place in the gardener's shed in the Rock Gardens and also in the pavilion at the bowling-greens on the recreation ground.

Roller-skating was very popular at that time, and we spent hours skating along the Embankment. It was even more fun starting alongside the Town Arms, gliding down the hill to the River Trent.

On leaving school I worked on Traffic Street and one day whilst walking to the office a railway horse and dray were parked alongside the pavement, the horse turned its head and took a chunk out of my jacket, and even though I wrote a letter of complaint, nothing was done. Today they'd be sued!

When I was younger, every Sunday we'd take a walk somewhere – Colwick Weir, or take the ferry (it cost a penny from the Suspension Bridge to the Becket School) and walk through the fields to Wilford. Sometimes we'd take the bus to Edwalton, walk across the fields and come back along Tollerton Lane and back to Bridgford. Then there was cycling – to Clifton to pick cowslips and bluebells.

And what our mothers had to put up with! Dad used to light a fire under the old copper every Monday morning, and hang the clothes-line outside in the backyard. If it rained we'd have sheets hanging in the living-room when we got home and of course the ironing was done on the kitchen table with a blanket for a cover – even after we bought mother an electric iron, mum still insisted on using the old flat-irons – she wasn't keen on electricity at all. She used to blacklead the old grate and the stove – until they were replaced by newer models, and the front doorstep was always scrubbed.

I remember the floods too in 1947 – down the yard we'd go to the toilet wearing our wellies. Everybody seemed a lot happier in those days even though there was very little money. At Christmas it was a *Rupert* annual, a box of chocolates and a few odds and ends, but we were quite content and never expected more.

I guess it's only natural, but I've often wondered over the years what became of my old schoolfriends and the kids in the neighbourhood – and not to forget the people I worked with.

Those were the days, and thank you for bringing it all back so clearly.

Mrs Iris Crouse (née Price), Canada

The Globe Cinema in more affluent times as it stood on the junction of Arkwright Street and London Road, which is to the right of the picture. (photograph: Geoffrey Oldfield)

Irene Hardman with her new born baby Laurie in the pram in the backyard at Bertram Street in 1959; and Irene pictured with husband John at the back door of their Meadows home.

In Praise of the Leeny Gang

The Meadows was fantastic. We had a great time there growing up. My brother, sister and I belonged to a gang called the Leeny Gang, and oh what times we all shared! Playing on bombed buildings and on top of coal heaps, then after that it was time to go in, to listen to *Dick Barton*. We couldn't miss that! Then we would all go to the picture houses like the Globe or Imperial to see anything from the musicals to the cowboys.

We lived in Bertram Street, just off Crocus Street and the neighbours were great! We were all brought up together everybody helping each other. Nobody had any money, but we had something money couldn't buy, great memories of great times!

I only wish I could take a slice of that and give some to the younger generation.

Even now after all these years we still see each other and have a good laugh about all those things we used to get up to.

Nothing could compare to all that! But then again us from The Meadows were special, well, we all think so! And we were proud to have been just a part of it. So thanks one and all for the Leeny Gang and for making my childhood a very special one!

Irene Hardman (née Lynch)

Idyllic Days at Iremonger Pond

I left school Easter 1937 and at the time I was living next door to the ordnance factory, on Middle Furlong Road. Solid-built homes, no bathrooms, but they could easily have been adapted. I went down one day after moving to Carlton and I stood and wept. My home was partially demolished, the lovely tiled fire-grates I had had installed were visible up on the bedroom level. I loved that house, having moved from Morrison's Terrace, Essex Street about 1936. On the terrace opposite my home lived the James family. A lovely family, cheerful, clean, mum, dad and family of boys; Dennis, now moved back to Nottingham from Cromer. We started school together at Launder Street (off Deering Street-Kirkewhite Street) around 1928. It was a tiny school with partitions between each class. Dennis had three other brothers, Ronnie and Stan being two of them.

Next door to the James's were George and Annie Marsden; opposite – the Sissons family, Reg, Joan, Alice, Frank (now dead), Alf, Herbert, Kate, Robert and Winnie. I wonder where they are now? I was actually born in Hope Street and my dad worked down Clifton Pit. He kept a few pigs and chickens and mum would sell eggs via the shop downstairs that we lived above.

So many very happy memories, but hard times. At the top of the terrace was the corner shop – my great-gran (Mrs Filewood) kept it and my great-aunt (Mrs Moore). They moved to Carlton Hill and the Haslams took over (the first car in the street!). The West family lived next to the shop, Jim, Mary, Rene and my best friend, Eric Statham who also has died. Is there anyone around who remembers these lovely people from Essex Street – the Cornellies, Len Kendrick and Meakin's sweet and grocery shop? Remember Mundall's chip shop – sit-in peas and chips for $1\frac{1}{2}$ d? The pot shop? The cheeky notes around the window display.

An aunt's brother in Kirkewhite Street ran for election for Labour, I gave out red banners. We sang 'Vote, vote, vote for Tom Cobley' but then fights ensued with the Blues, represented I believe by Ernest Stedham!

Then I recall fishing at Iremonger's Pond over the Halfpenny Bridge when I caught a pike on a Woolworth's rod. All the men came running to help. The manager from Flittermans stores liked my dad, so I too was privileged to picnic in his huge tent by the pond. Afterwards, watching over their gear at the Ferry Inn where they had a penny farthing bike, and apple trees and a talking parrot. I loved it there.

Irene Bedford (née Roome)

Pinching Precious Moments with the Boys

Although I wasn't born in The Meadows I spent most of my teens down there with my best mate Joyce Bacon. I still see Joyce as we both still live in Beeston. Joyce had a grandad who lived down The Meadows. He was a great big man towering over us but so gentle and lovely. He was called Dockum, that's the only name everyone knew him as.

I also remember going down to help him clear up after the 1947 floods, but that was an excuse to see the lads we used to meet at the Imperial picture house. The lads I remember were Barry Worrel, Jackie Fox, Allen Mullering and his cousin whose name I can't remember, Owen Green and my happy time spent down there with the likes of Doris O'Dell or her family. Also the laughs Joyce and I had flying over Wilford Bridge hoping to catch the bus in time to get back to Beeston as we had to be home by ten or we couldn't go out next week.

Mrs Sheila Oldham

Playtime at the New Pad

The houses were two-up and two-down where I lived on Newcastle Road. There was

The all girls school of Queen's Walk Junior around 1934. The headmaster was Mr Wilkinson, and the form teacher was Miss Hurd.

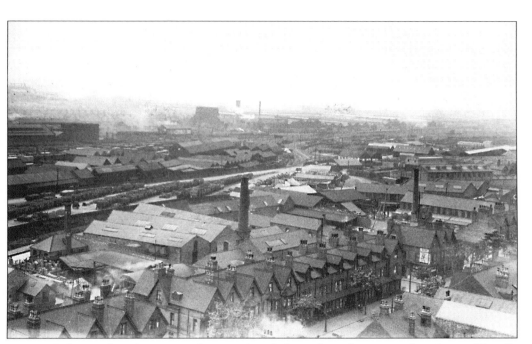

A view of The Meadows from Nottingham Castle with the smoke and towers marking Cammell Laird's (the Royal Ordnance plant known as the gun factory locally) in the background, and the houses of Castle Boulevard in the foreground. (photograph: F.W. Stevenson)

a rather odd, large family house, one was called the Green House as it was always painted green, the other was where the Sheriff of Nottingham lived, a Mr Williamson, that made us very posh.

At the bottom of the street was a dead end as the gun factory ran along it. There were two shops, a beer-off and a cobbler's, a Mr Wagstaff.

I went to Queen's Walk School and if you went there you were a quick walker and a slow runner. If you went to Bosworth Road you were a boz-eyed kipper. In winter you could go to the play centre at night on Bosworth Road.

We had a long way to school, it took about half an hour, there were no buses or school buses and we did this four times a day.

I enjoyed my childhood in The Meadows. You could play in the street or on the Tips, go for a walk along New Pad, or along the Trent.

Mrs K. Lockwood

Fit for a Prince

An event I remember quite well took place on 1 August 1923 when HRH the Prince of Wales visited Nottingham to review the pupils of the schools of the city. We (pupils of London Road School) were taken by train from the Midland Station to Carrington which was then at the end of Gregory Boulevard, and we walked to the Forest. We were given a souvenir

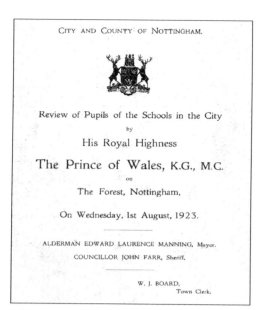

CITY AND COUNTY OF NOTTINGHAM.

Review of Pupils of the Schools in the City

by

His Royal Highness

The Prince of Wales, K.G., M.C.

on

The Forest, Nottingham,

On Wednesday, 1st August, 1923.

ALDERMAN EDWARD LAURENCE MANNING, Mayor.

COUNCILLOR JOHN FARR, Sheriff.

W. J. BOARD,
Town Clerk.

The programme to commemorate the visit of the Prince of Wales to Nottingham in 1923, still in the proud possession of Lily Hooley.

programme of the procedure. While the prince was in Nottingham he also visited Ellerslie House to see the wounded soldiers.

I also remember during my last year at London Road being taken to sit on the stand of Notts County Football Club for a lesson. My teacher at that time was Miss Robinson. I was born in 1913 in The Meadows and attended London Road from 1916-1924.

L. Hooley

Tragedy Amidst the Rush to Grow Up

As a child growing up in The Meadows area from the middle of the1930s, Crocus Street was my stamping-ground. We were among

The London Road Junior School, class of 1918. Lily Hooley is first from the right in the third row. The teachers were Miss Earnes, to the left of group, and Miss Donnelly, to the right.

neighbours who helped each other along. Godber's factory was across the road and through the side street we could see London Road Junior School.

My mother bringing me up alone had to work and so she arranged for my meals at a butcher's shop across the road from the school. What a joy it was to see Mr Holiday, the owner of the shop, sending the sausage meat whizzing into their skins. They also had a dog, Bobbie, and as I grew older I was allowed to take him for a walk. One day venturing onto London Road, I had let the dog off the lead, he disappeared into Hickings coal-hole. I started to run, panic-stricken, down the road when a voice hailed me and a man with Bobbie unhurt, but very

Little Shirley Watts in the arms of her mother, Alice Parkin, on Crocus Street in 1936, the year Shirley was born. Behind is St Margaret's church.

Shirley in her pram in the Crocus Street backyards.

dirty, brought him out.

Other events left a sad memory, when the six-year-old daughter of a neighbour drowned in the River Trent. Water was a great temptation to us children with the Trent, the River Leen and the canal so near to us. Mum took me to see this little angel laid out, telling me I would never be afraid of seeing anyone dead again. Monica had been taken from the water before being bitten by the rats and so was unmarked. What a tragedy, our street grieved along with the family.

Money was tight and many families had trading cheques to obtain major items like furniture, carpets and clothes. The Meadows

A generation earlier in The Meadows finds Shirley's mum the baby, on the knee of her own mother Mrs Taylor in 1904.

area had small shops on almost every street corner, the grocer's, greengrocer's, fish and chip shop, beer-off, and cobbler's, all were there only a few yards away. For many it was the normal thing to run up a bill and settle it at the weekend.

It was a time when some of us made rag rugs as a pastime, but some homes would be hard pressed to have even such a floor covering.

Many of the young men were away serving in the forces at that time and to aid the war effort a paper drive was held by the schools. Children were asked to bring papers and magazines, the more weight collected, so the child was awarded a badge, going through the ranks until reaching General or Field Marshal. The top collectors were invited to the Council House for tea. I can't remember what we ate that day, only the sight of dozens of children climbing the staircase in the Council House to have their tea.

Then came VE Day 1945 and the street parties.

Our kitchen was so small that the sink, a boiler in the corner, and a cooker, filled it to capacity with hardly room to turn round, with a shelf above being the only place to store kitchen implements. At about eleven years old I had the desire, along with a friend, to have a pet mouse, so we bought one each. Unknown to my mum I put them on our kitchen shelf in a container with air holes, they weren't there long though, as my mum had a keen nose for mice, living where we did, and made me part with them double-quick. The boy around the corner eagerly becoming their new owner.

Before having a tiled fireplace we had the black leaded type with the oven at the side. The 'black clocks' certainly loved the warmth. I dreaded opening the cupboard at

the side where they lived.

While the war was on I remember Godber's factory having a fire. It made the paint on our front door bubble, but we children had a great time sorting through the charred cotton reels afterwards. When the sirens went to signal an air raid Mum and I would stay at home, we never wanted to go in the shelters around the corner. We would take cover under the stairs in the pantry, removing the mousetraps first, of course.

I would be interested to know when the Crocus Street houses were built as my mother had been brought up in the house as part of a large family, only leaving for a short time on her marriage then coming back to live in the house. I offer my tribute to all who struggled then from a lack of money, the men who tried to raise vegetables and flowers on allotments, the mothers who kept children and homes clean when it really was hard work in those days.

Shirley Watts

Hello Dolly Tub and Here Come the Wash-Day Blues

After I was born at No. 14 Kinglake Street in my maternal grandparents' house on 14 March 1928, we lived for a short while in Queen's Road, Beeston and then moved to a flat over a fish and chip shop which used to be in Bathley Street, The Meadows. The shop was owned by Mrs Green and my mother used to help her. Strange to say the houses where the fish and chip shop was were all demolished in the levellings of the 1970s but those on the opposite side of Bathley Street are still there.

In the summer of 1931 we moved to

No. 178 Waterway Street and my parents lived there for twenty-eight years and brought up a family of five on very low income so as we grew up we found all sorts of ways to supplement that income. I would climb into derelict factories through broken windows and search for scrap metal and take it to Tricket's scrap-yard at Colwick and sometimes we would pick up more scrap on waste ground at the bottom of Meadow Lane. Opposite our house on Waterway Street was Reader's old iron foundry with huge double doors and iron-framed windows either side of it, minus the glass, smashed out by vandals.

Using the sloping ornamental brickwork under those windows we would climb up and get through the frames and drop down to the black sand floor and rake through the sand to find rusty old tools and pieces of iron. We would also climb the iron ladders up to a gantry high up near the roof where the rusting crane still stood with its long chains, climb out onto the crane and down the chains, down to the hook and swing back and forth. As a result showers of rust and dust would fall around us and then we would drop the 10ft or so to the sand, sending up clouds of dust. We would be absolutely filthy.

Lord knows how our mothers got our clothes clean again. Remember everything had to be washed by hand, in a dolly tub in the yard using a 'ponch', which was either a three-legged stool on a pole with a T-handle or an upside-down funnel with holes on it so the water would be forced up and through the dirty washing.

There was a boiler in a corner of the scullery, which consisted of a large iron bowl in a brick surround with a fire-grate underneath it. This sometimes took an age to light and when the wind was in the wrong direction it filled the house with smoke. Us kids sometimes used the wooden boiler lid as a shield in mock battles. Mum didn't think much to that, especially when I buried an axe head in it a time or two.

I hated wash-days, when we came home from school the house would smell of damp washing and a clothes-horse would be round the fireplace and clothes steaming away and in winter that was no joke.

From the yard of that old foundry, we used to get through a gap in the fence and go into the factory next door, Lee & Hunt's Engineering Works, and we would pretend to make things on the machines. In those days all the machines were driven by overhead belts run on a single gas engine.

I left Trent Bridge School for senior boys at Easter 1942. Last time I saw it, it was a YTS training centre and it still looked as it did when I left. The iron bars were still in front of the windows where we used to swing and turn somersaults and I cracked my head by running into one of them. At least something in The Meadows hasn't changed much.

My first job was at Redgate's Iron Foundry. I got the job because Mr Redgate was an old boyfriend of my mother's and they set me on as a core-maker at 15s a week, for which I worked 56 hours, this included Saturday mornings. Now and again they allowed me to do simple moulding in sand-boxes which I found quite interesting. One of my tasks was to go to the local chippy at lunch time and collect fish and chips for the other chaps' lunches or ham cobs from one of the corner shops on Waterway Street. One day my carrier bike wheel was run over and squashed by an LMS horse-drawn dray. I asked the blokes whose lunch I had collected to help me to pay for the repairs and they refused. I had to borrow the money from my father and pay him back at a shilling a week and since I only received 2s 6d for myself from my wages, that came a bit hard. I told the other guys in the foundry that I would not fetch their lunch ever again, so it wasn't long before I was given my 'release' from that job. It was wartime and it wasn't easy to give someone the sack then.

Ken Jackson

'Marathon' Woman of Old Welbeck Vintage

Our family (of West Indian origin) consisting of my mother, father and five children lived at No. 48 Waterway Street up until 1977, when we moved to Manifold Gardens in the new Meadows. I attended the old Welbeck School and also the new one (not many kids can say that). The old Welbeck was situated on Kinglake Street. What a wonderful school that was, with its dark wooden floors, cream walls, high ceilings etc. Mr Howitt was the headmaster and my immediate teacher was Mrs Thorpe. I'll always remember her with her long black hair with centre parting and she always wore black gloves with rings worn over the gloves! Also Mr Smith, he was a newly-qualified teacher (I found this out in 1990 when I organized a mini infant school re-union and was able to trace Mr Smith who to my delight was willing to attend). On one swimming lesson at Portland Baths he fell in the pool fully clothed! Boy, I'll never forget that, it was the talk of the school.

Across from the school on Kinglake Street was the 'Miller's shop' where we used to get our jublees, drumsticks, fruit salads,

CITY OF NOTTINGHAM EDUCATION COMMITTEE

TRENT BRIDGE SECONDARY SCHOOL
FOR BOYS

SPEECH DAY

Thursday, 13th December, 1956, at 7 p.m,

in

BRIDGEWAY HALL

The Address will be given by
W. G. JACKSON, Esq., B.A., M.Ed.
(Director of Education)

Chairman
COUNCILLOR R. E. GREEN (The Sheriff of Nottingham)
(Chairman of the School Governors)

The speech day programme for Trent Bridge Boys' School in 1956.

blackjacks etc. Oh! How I wish I could go back to those days!

I remember playing 'two-balls' on Waterway Street with my friends. Throwing balls over the cars, you had to be quick otherwise you'd lose your ball under the step that would go down to the cellar, as they went by. Constantly asking for the time as I couldn't dare let my father return home from work to find me 'playing out', as I'd be punished, usually with the buckle end of the belt.

I remember the Liptons shop on Waterway Street – they used to call me 'the Marathon (Snickers) girl', as I was forever in there buying them. Their daughter, Kathleen, was in my class at school. They had an Alsatian that bit me on my arm! I remember thinking that I was going to die!

I have vivid memories of my sister and myself climbing on the window mesh at Furse, looking at the young lads working. Furse was directly opposite our house. There are so many, many families I remember from Waterway Street namely – the Leaps (who lived next door), the Glovers, the Ashleys, the Atwells, the Mugglestones, the Fowlers and the Smarts to name but a few.

Waterway Street will always have a special place in my heart and I am pleased that part of it is still standing. In the past I have returned and stood in front of Furse, closed my eyes and relived my childhood, treasured memories.

Cargel Foreman (née Green)

Compassion on Your Doorstep

The area near Waterway Street, between Arkwright Street and London Road where I was born in 1938, provided many fond memories. I suppose my first one was of heading for the air-raid shelters in Lammas Street when I was about five years old. In my innocence, it proved quite exciting with no in-built fear of such things as bombs, bullets and killing, with everyone huddled together in shared dread and anticipation.

During and after the war, strict rationing was in force but with my father being a miner down Clifton Colliery, we had such things as butter, meat, cheese and coal supplied when most people were struggling with such things that were termed as luxuries. It was a time of great compassion and comradeship, neighbours being real neighbours and everyone helping one another to survive.

After the war was over, my youth was spent at London Road Infants' School and then at the infamous Trent Bridge School on the Embankment where many lifelong friendships were forged. I will never forget the envy I felt at the 'rich' youths going to Mundella School, getting the education that I thought I deserved, but, because my parents lacked money I was denied the chance to become educated to doctorate level. My ambition was to be a doctor or perhaps a barrister or lawyer serving the great British people.

Having moved some thirty years ago south of the River Trent to 'bread and lard island' (West Bridgford), memories of The Meadows keep flooding back to my misspent youth and the happy relationships that were moulded there, and the friendliness and happiness of the people.

It will always stick in my mind the time when one of the presenters of *Two-Way Family Favourites* on reading a letter from Germany to someone in the Meadows stated that the address was Crocus Street, The Meadows, Nottingham and saying 'What a beautiful place it sounded'. How right she was, and how true it was in the happy days before developers and wreckers of dreams moved in. But progress cannot stand still, I only hope the next generation is offered the same opportunities that we in The Meadows had.

Brian Blythe

From Sir – with Fond Memories

I was a teacher at Queen's Walk Junior School (later to become Welbeck School), Queen's Drive in The Meadows from 1949 to 1966.

Queen's Walk football team of 1950s vintage; Derrick Moore is the teacher on the left at the back.

They were very happy years. The children were super and I have very fond memories of them, their parents and the school. The Meadows was a close-knit community with parents very supportive of the school and its firm discipline. Not that many children had to be disciplined, they generally did as they were told immediately, so despite classes of forty-eight, teaching, I'm sure, was nowhere near as difficult as it is today.

Inevitably, there was plenty of class teaching, especially in history, geography, scripture (now religious education) and formal writing lessons. But there was grouping for maths, reading and spelling.

To take spelling as an example, this evolved into twelve groups of four – with twenty words to learn each week. Certainly in this class, finding the four were not really a group at all, and making use of 'testing in pairs' each individual child built up a list of 'words I need to learn'. Words were added to this list (providing I thought they were at a suitable level of difficulty) from their compositions (creative writing as it later became). So it was not all 'chalk and talk'.

Derrick Moore

31

Above: *Staff at Queen's Walk School in 1955; Derrick Moore is standing on the far right.*
Below: *pupils in a class photograph around 1956.*

The first Essex portable apparatus to be used in the county was at Queen's Walk School. Brand new in the 1950s.

Daredevils of the 'Bullring'

My mother's name was Mallott and she was born at the top end of Woolmer Road. My father was born on Glapton Road. Both grandfathers were engine-drivers on the LMS railway. I was born on 11 January 1924 at No. 122 Woolmer Road.

Names I recall are Toulson's (the pork-butchers), Timson's (the bakers), and the Shirebrook pub. People who lived in Woolmer Road were the Inkleys, Peppers, Wakelings, Boyce, Eyot and Mrs Smith who lived at No. 120.

I started school at Collygate School where we had slates and chalk and sat on the floor! Then on to Trent Bridge Juniors' – anyone remember Miss Appleton? She also taught my mother. From there, I went to Trent Bridge Senior Boys' School. I did not make Mundella School, not bright enough.

Here are some of the teachers' names: Mr Syson (arithmetic), Mr Smith (handy with the cane), Mr Curry (French and handy with the three-thronged strap), Mr English (art), Mr Richards (geography), Mr Lawrence (deputy head and brilliant teacher) and finally Mr Barton Hart (music and also a very good teacher).

How many are still with us I wonder? I would be delighted to know, because I am over seventy-five years old! I also was a choirboy at St Faith's church, Bathley Street for many years. The organist was Mr Skull, the vicar being the Revd Belcher and then Revd Inglis. Life could be fun and rough in The Meadows. On the bottom of Woolmer

It was a penny admission when motion pictures were shown at the Bridgeway Hall, pictured here in the 1930s. (photograph: Nottingham Evening Post)

Road was the Rec'. We played 'kick-about', cricket and chased the girls at haymaking.

Then there was the 'Bullring'. This was a circle around the bowling-green, wire-fenced and hedged. We used to race our home-made trolleys round it, and those of us who had bikes raced dirt-track style, trying to copy the speedway riders at Colwick Park.

Ray Murcott

Pram Ride to Fetch the Coke

Coming from a family of ten, I have such happy memories of The Meadows. One was taking my brother Billie's suit to be cleaned or pressed every week at Clean and Press Well on Queen's Road. He would give me one shilling a week and that would pay for my Friday night pictures. I also recall going to the Penny Pictures, at the Bridgeway Hall every Tuesday. Marvellous. We were never bored unlike the children of today. On summer days, all the kids would play in the River Leen, often making dams with old bricks and seaweed, so it would be deep enough for us to swim in. Looking down at our legs we would have bloodsuckers stuck on them. Summer nights, everyone would be sitting out on the fronts of the houses. You would see old Frank fetching his ale in a gallon jug. It was so nice, even the grown-ups would have a game at playing skipping with you. Games like 'crumbs and crusts', 'hop charge', 'tin lurky', hop scotch, snobs, whip and top, skating and hide-and-seek – such variety and such fun. Mr Cope was known for taking his horse up and down Bertram Street many, many times for his exercise, and fetching Mr Hallam's taxi every night. Everyone was known to each other in the neighbourhood. Coming from a big family was good, but so sad when we lost our parents.

I was just four years old when I lost my dad, and eleven when Mum died, so my sister, Joyce, looked after us all and she did a marvellous job. In winter, we would take it in turns to fetch coke every Saturday morning, queuing up for what seemed hours (often pushing old broken-down prams, with buckled wheels). If at the end we found that they had sold out of coke, then it was off to Robin Hood Street to fetch coal bricks. Sometimes folk would make their own coal bricks out of slack and old sugar bags.

Mrs B. Parker

Bombed by the Kaiser's Zeppelin

When I was about five years old I went to live at No. 60 Queen's Walk. Now aged ninety-two, I perhaps have more memories of The Meadows than most!

Queen's Walk was really beautiful but it wasn't the same after they took the iron railings for scrap iron during the war. Times were very hard but we all helped one another. I attended Queen's Walk School, which was just the other side of 'the Cricket' from us, as our back entrance was on Kirkewhite Street. We had a big open space and all the backyards went off it. The wall to Launder Street School, also to Launder Cottages, came to our back, and all the

neighbours hung the washing there. It got very muddy on wet days as it wasn't paved but it was a great place for us kids to play. Trent Bridge School was taken over for wounded soldiers, so we had to share our school one week in the mornings then one week afternoons. I remember the Zeppelin coming over in 1916. It bombed some houses on Crocus Street and damaged the Midland Station clock, also Woolworths store near the water fountain. My father was in the trenches in France and fighting on the Somme. Parker's was a shop I recall on the corner of Launder Street from which I would fetch twopenny packets of Woodbines and if you didn't have twopence, they would sell one cigarette and a match for a halfpenny. All our walks and picnics were by the Trent. I must have walked round the Embankment hundreds of times, wheeling a baby as I had three brothers and three sisters younger and one brother older so there was always a baby in the family. Then there were the cinemas we went to on Saturday afternoons for twopence. They were silent, and someone played the piano.

Everything was transported by horse and cart – milk, bread, goods from the railways. Wednesday was lady's day at Trent Baths. Across the Trent were Willow Woods and the trees hung over into the river, it was so lovely. Before the Memorial Gardens were built on the Embankment, there was a farm where us kids went potato picking for sixpence a day.

I went to Mundella School when I was eleven years old, just when the war finished and later married in 1930, at St George's church. My husband was born on Walnut Tree Lane and he worked at Boots, Island Street for forty-five years.

Florence Broad (née Revill)

Resplendent in 1903, the Queen's Walk amidst which little Florence Revill grew up, complete with iron railings before they were dismantled for scrap metal during the war.

Tips, Pad and Tales from the Riverbank

We had so many places to play. Wilford Bridge which we called Halfpenny Bridge, was one. We would swim on the other side and play by the side of the power station and Clifton Pit. At the back of the pit were swamps and wasteland called the Tips. I remember when the swamps were frozen, we had been to collect coal from the pit. The ice melted and the barrow fell in the water – what a laugh. Alongside the Royal Ordnance Factory was a path we called Pad. We often went out for the day with a bottle of water and some jam sandwiches.

At the top end of the factory was a police hut and we asked them to fill our bottle with water. Sometimes we would collect blackberries that were growing on the inside of the railings. Then down Lenton Lane, the River Leen used to run under a bridge, we called it White Bridge, we would build a dam so we could swim in it – such happy days.

During the 1947 floods I lived on King's Meadow Road. I was nine years old. The Salvation Army came in a boat to feed us. Also tanks came down our street and gave the children a ride but they would shake the houses so much our front room fireplace fell in and we had to have a new one.

I will always remember the good times we had and also the many friends and neighbours from those happy days.

Mrs V. Stafford (née Hart)

Streetwise Recollections

I was five when I first came to live in The Meadows in 1918. We lived on Hawthorne Street facing the Bosworth Road School as it was called then, near the Trent and the Clifton Pit. Around this area were a lot of allotments. People had pigs and poultry and round and about there were fields called 'crocus fields' because of the flowers growing there.

We moved to a smaller street called Peg Street, close to the Salvation Army. On Sunday, if anyone passed away, they would march round the streets playing the *Death March*. All the streets led to other terraces

Vera Hart's grandmother, with Vera's father Tom (far right) and her uncle, pictured at the turn of the century when the family had moved to No. 96 King's Meadow Road.

Vera, kneeling in the middle of the picture, part of a dance class at Bosworth Road School that performed before Princess Elizabeth on The Forest in 1949.

and Middle Furlong Road led to the gun factory, the railway also ran alongside. We had lamplighters and 'knockers-up', these being men who worked down the pit. I recall we seemed to have lots of fun, bonfires on the Fifth of November with simple fireworks and on Empire Day there was a maypole for the children.

Whips, tops, shuttlecocks, marbles, we were quite happy with the simple things. May Day, we were lucky if we were picked to go on a dray and taken round the streets waving streamers.

Peg Street led on to Goodhead where another entry led on to Rupert Street. All met up with Wilford Road where there were shops each side of the road. The Meadow Dairy, Marsden's, Home and Colonial, two chemists, shoe shop, the Imperial Picture House (sixpence a time), chip shops (fish and chips sixpence). You could even spend a farthing on an everlasting strip. Trams were running, the fare being halfpenny to the Walter Fountain, one penny to the market.

After the trams came the trolleybuses, which ran from the terminus to the top of the Wells Road. Kirkewhite Street led onto Queen's Drive, a lovely tree-lined road, which went up from the River Trent to Midland Station with lots of large bay window houses – quite select.

On King's Meadow Road, they gave away soup to the poor people when the miners went on strike. I also remember a shop on Wilford Road where breakfast was free. There were bad times as well as good.

It was funny during elections when yellow Liberal streamers, red for Labour, blue for the Tories were seen everywhere. Woe betide if you came across the opposition!

At Christmas we made our own trimmings and were quite happy with a stocking in which there was an apple, orange, sugar pig and a few nuts. Then we'd have a lovely dinner. My mum made her own puds, ginger-beer, herb-beer and home-made wine. Yes, I loved every minute that I lived in The Meadows.

Vera Daynes (née Wattan)

Eternally Grateful for a Life Saved and Full of Happiness

Many of my memories have laid dormant for half a century. One that has never left me, however, was when Vera and I were walking by the canal off Wilford Road when my foot slipped on the slime and I fell into one of the foaming sluice-gates. When I surfaced Vera grabbed my hand and hauled me out. To this day I don't know where she found the strength, her being smaller than me. I have owed my life to this very special friend Vera Hart. I think she must know how fond I am of her. We both got a clout from our mums on arriving home for being near the canal in the first place.

My parents ran the Shipstone's off-licence on the corner of King's Meadow Road and Castleton Street from 1943 to 1953. The shop was a busy one catching the trade of the workers going to and from the gun factory; the enormous Shipstone's dray-horses used to deliver the barrels of beer weekly, what a sight they were. During the floods the barrels used to float around the cellar. Worrying times for the adults but great fun for us children. No school, fishing from the bedroom windows, swans swimming up the street. We had some great characters come in the shop, some we had nicknames for because mum didn't know their real names. One lady

Little Vera Hart, on the left, and Margaret Bromhead, whose life Vera saved by hauling her out of the canal, pictured at the back of their houses in the King's Meadow Road.

used to bring in a kettle for her pint of ale but the majority had very nice jugs. We sold by the measure, for this, customers would bring in a cup. I would help to weigh the sugar into those blue bags and help out generally. I loved it.

The Salvation Army would stand underneath the gas lamp on our corner Sunday evenings, always an enjoyable event. Quite a number of people would join in the singing.

Playing whip and top, two-balls, skipping, rounders, blind-man's buff, dobbie catch me if you can, walking down the Pad and onto Long Lane, picking wild flowers or blackberries, shuffling through the fallen leaves in autumn down on the Embankment and of course roller-skating. The latter pastime brings to mind Mo of the later

famed Roly-Polys. She came to live on King's Meadow Road, her rollers were attached to lovely white boots and her skating was good.

Ted Brown was our next-door neighbour. He had two children, Raymond and Veronica. I remember Veronica being born. Ted must have been a driver, as I recall a very heavily-laden lorry of timber occasionally parked outside his house.

In 1949 I went to Trent Bridge School, walking the distance twice a day. I made another lifelong friend there with whom I am still in touch.

My childhood, along with all your other readers, was certainly full of happy days.

Margaret Lilley (née Bromhead)

39

A Regal Touch

I had the happiest of times as a child growing up in The Meadows living on Wilford Road. They were made all the better by attending Queen's Walk School for Girls. It was truly a wonderful school. I still see some old pupils and former classmates like Rita Schloss but I'd love to see more. They really were the most delightful days.

Gladys Hull

The Pleasure was all Mine

Agnes Street, just off Arkwright Street was the place of my birth. I went to Trent Bridge School until I was ten years old then we left to live on Talbot Street, but I was always down The Meadows as my older sister lived on Waterway Street. The Meadows was like a little town of its own. Arkwright Street was a wonderful shopping centre, you could buy just about anything. We also had four cinemas, the Globe at Trent Bridge, the Grove on Kirkewhite Street, the Imperial on Wilford Road and the Queen's at the top of Arkwright Street, near the Midland Station.

Some of my early memories are at the end of the war. We kids would go to Bridgeway Hall and watch Penny Pictures. Later it was Twopenny Talkers, we would sit, lined up on benches, and watch the silent movies absolutely fascinated with them all. In the school holidays, you could go to Bridgeway Hall and get a bowl of soup and a chunk of bread for about twopence.

Class 3A of the Queen's Walk School for girls in 1931/32, fondly remembered by Gladys Hull, who is standing fourth from the right in the third row from the front.

Trent Bridge School, class of 1950. Yvonne Luckett is third from the left in the second row from the front. Her teacher was Miss Allwood and the headmaster was Mr Gibson.

The people were not very well off, but the spirit of the folks was brilliant, everyone helped one another. If an elderly person on the street was ill, we kids were sent to do their shopping, and the mums all rallied round and did their cleaning and washing and so forth.

My auntie and uncle lived at the Pleasure Park at Colwick. Mum and I would catch a boat on the Embankment and for a few pence had a lovely ride on the river. Dropped off at the Pleasure Park, we enjoyed a day playing in the sand, going on the swings and slot machines. It was like being on holiday.

My auntie and uncle were badly flooded in 1947 as were a lot of The Meadows, especially those who lived near the Embankment.

I still visit down there as my godmother and father live on Green Street facing my old school, Trent Bridge. Every time I go to see them, I look at the school playground and it brings back so many memories.

Yvonne Keeling (née Luckett)

Backstreet boys and girls near King's Meadow Road. These pictures were taken in the late 1960s but are evidence of the back to back housing and communal outside toilets that had survived for almost a century.

CHAPTER 2

The People

A wartime Meadows wedding outside Queen's Drive church, April 1944. Gladys Barnes has just been married to Mr Leslie Walters. Also pictured are Mr and Mrs Barnes, Miss B. Brindley, Mr Walters senior, Les's brother and E. Barnes in uniform.

A View from the Inside

Mention the old Meadows and you normally get two different points of view. To outsiders who did not live there it was a dirty, poor, deprived area with back to back housing with outside loos and no bathrooms. Packed with rough people. The whole area needed knocking down and its people rehoused.

However to the folk who lived there it was a special community where they lived, worked and played. A place where neighbours helped each other, doors could be left open and children were watched by all and sundry. It was a place full of character, whose names still live on. Tricky Dick the poacher, who charged fourpence a rabbit and was very much in demand during the war years, when rationing was in force. Dolly his wife who always wore a moth-eaten fox fur collar on her evening visits to the local pub. Gypsy Smith of Essex Street. The local abortionist who did a roaring trade, especially when the Americans came here. The two prostitutes who lived on Midland Crescent who often gave pennies to us local kids. Of course as children we did not know their profession. Parents were very moral in those days and such things were never discussed in front of their children.

The shopkeepers on Wilford Road, who knew all their customers by first names. Joe Turner, the butcher, Miss Sanderson of the tripe shop, Frank Simmonds the pot man with his window full of saucy ditties and the sounds of laughter as he told his rather doubtful tales to his customers. Mr Jorden the pork-butcher who so intrigued the youngsters. We used to gaze through his shop window at this very portly man. Never ever could a human being so resemble his produce. Frank Price the greengrocer, Towlson's, another pork-butcher, Marsden's, Home and Colonial, Battersby's the cobblers and two pawnshops where suits and other best clothes were taken on a Monday and redeemed on pay-day.

Clifton Pit and the clatter of miners' boots on the cobble-stones as they went to the early morning shift returning with black sooty faces. No pit baths in those days. Just the tin bath which hung outside and water boiled in the copper.

The gun factory which employed hundreds of people working on munitions during the war. At 5 p.m. the King's Meadow Road was a heaving mass of workers dashing to catch the buses waiting on Hawthorne Street. They actually let disabled people out a few minutes early to enable them to get a head start from the

crush. The war, blackout and air-raid shelters. Everyone was allocated a place. Ours was on the Tips. There were about twelve in all, the last being about 12ft from the perimeter fence of the gun factory. People today would never tolerate this, we would have public meetings, action groups and general disruption but in the 1930s and 1940s working class folk did not question authority, they did as they were told. So as soon as the sirens went we were plucked from our beds, dressed and rushed across to the shelters for safety! Once inside we either occupied a bunk or huddled round a smelly little stove. The rows that occurred were a nightly affair with parents all trying to secure a place near the heat for their children. I can't imagine why, it was certainly no warmer there, all I can remember is lots and lots of smoke billowing out, people coughing, eyes running.

You could only see the people next to you, so children cried and parents argued to be quickly stopped as soon as the planes went over. I can remember vividly the air-raid warden saying, 'Hark, listen, shshsh', so we all duly ducked and were only allowed to whisper. To this day, over fifty years on, I wish someone could explain why this ritual occurred, but throughout the war years, whether at home, in the pantry, or in a shelter, when planes went overhead we whispered – children and adults alike.

After the war came the bad winter of 1946-1947. Collecting coal from the slag heaps behind the swamps. Clutching our little bags of pebble-sized nuggets, running home as if we had found gold. The 1947 floods, when the Trent overflowed, dirty water swirling around the streets. Milk and bread delivered by boat, hoisted to upstairs rooms by ropes and buckets.

Voting days when children ran around

with streamers fighting with the opposition. As a very large Labour stronghold the few children with the blue Conservative were very easy targets and many fights and bruised shins were the order of the day.

When The Meadows was demolished a community was gone, its people scattered but The Meadows' spirit still lingers on in the people who once lived there. A very special place with special people which to outsiders appears rather strange, but old Meadows folk know and understand, just ask them, they will tell you in great detail.

Joan Wilkinson (née Cornthorn)

Lucky to Have Been Part of It

Yes, I lived in The Meadows happily, in a small comfortable house. I was married rather late in life, almost forty in fact. We had a lovely, brand-new home, and every comfort. I found the people very friendly and caring. It was very convenient for my husband's work, a good shopping area and so near to the Trent Bridge, two minutes to a bus for the city centre and Bunbury Street, opposite my front door. I was on the Trent Embankment, weather permitting, most afternoons. Two minutes along I could be in the Memorial Gardens, but Hitler changed all that. We were bombed out of our cosy little house, but I can say I lived among very honest people. So many that night were injured, many more killed including young children. But I have now been on my own forty-four years, so you see I must be a very lucky lady to have such wonderful memories of The Meadows. My dear mam used to tell us, when she was a young girl she used to deliver the milk round on The Meadows by pony and trap before she went on to train to

Bill Hibbitt on his Co-op dairy round in The Meadows shortly after the Second World War. (photograph: J.B. Hibbitt)

be a tailoress. That must be 160 years or more now.

Mrs Elsie Bartles

Everything Just Dandy

I have many happy childhood memories of The Meadows as my father worked for the Nottingham Co-op Dairy and delivered milk in the area.

On summer weekends he would take me along to help him, first to the dairy on Meadow Lane to load the dray then down to the stables and upstairs to collect Dandy, a large black dray-horse. Once Dandy had come down the ramp I would hold his head

45

while my father 'clocked him on', each horse had its own clock card to record its hours on duty as well as a book that had to be signed every day for the nosebag.

My father didn't have to go far to begin his daily round, the houseboat moored by Victoria Embankment being the first call. From there it was right turn into Bunbury Street, Fraser Road, then up, down and along Pyatt, Turney, Bathley, Lamcote, Reacliffe, Muskham, Orange and Bell Street.

On Sunday mornings we had the streets to ourselves with just the aroma of breakfast bacon and later on the Sunday roast hanging over those quiet streets making our mouths water.

Grass grew between the Mountsorrel blocks that shot up to the road surface, and in some quiet corners it was long enough for Dandy to eat. Sometimes he would mount the pavement to munch someone's hedge and occasionally some old lady would give him a crust, then Dandy would reward her by leaving a small deposit outside her front gate. Out would come the bucket and dustpan and Dandy's deposit would no doubt end up keeping someone's rhubarb warm.

My father would buy the *Sunday Graphic* and his Park Drives from the corner shop, and when we arrived in Orange Street, if there was a large ice-cream cone hanging over No. 21's shop front, I knew there was just a chance dad would buy me a home-made ice-cream.

Dandy knew when we had finished the round and would set off at a trot towards Meadow Lane which on match days would be crowded with fans and maybe one or two policemen, everyone moved off the road to let our black charger through. Dandy wanted to get back to his stable and my dad

wanted to get to the Navigation for a well-earned pint. Happy days.

Mr J.B. Hibbitt

A Meadows Upbringing

The Meadows was home to me during my formative years having come into this world in Middle Furlong Road in May 1919. I went to Queen's Walk School and then transferred to Trent Bridge School in 1930.

I regularly attended the Queen's Walk Congregational Sunday school from the age of four until transferring to Mapperley in 1960, being scholar, teacher, secretary, etc., and being active in the church.

I joined the 90th Nottingham Scout Troop at the age of seven as a Cub and proceeded to take part in all Scout activities until being called into the Army in 1939.

Finally, my mother Mrs Emily Barnes helped to rescue a child from the River Trent near Wilford Toll Bridge in 1943 and received a commendation from the Royal Humane Society. She also took part in the *Nottingham Journal* 'Big Swim' round the Embankment in 1927.

Mr E.A. Barnes

Baker's Move to 'Bread and Lard Land'

Until 1941 when I became a member of 'bread and lard island' (West Bridgford) I was most definitely Meadows born and bred. Still am, of course. My father was a baker and had his own business. He was

The 90th Nottingham Scout troop, based in The Meadows, pictured in 1930 on the Queen's Walk cricket ground on the occasion of the wedding of Scoutmaster McClatchie (Skipper) to Miss Clark (Cub Mistress).

known locally as 'the midnight baker' because he used to deliver the bread very late, in his horse and cart.

Unfortunately, in 1926 he had a confrontation with an Austin 7 and that was the end of the delivery horse and cart and the business became motorized.

My father retired in 1937 but we still lived in the same house which was next door to Godber's cotton factory. However, in 1941, there was a disastrous fire there and it was burnt down and also the young night-watchman, aged thirty-four, lost his life in the blaze. Our property was also damaged, and we left The Meadows then, but I have many happy memories of life there.

St Margaret's church was situated just opposite our bakery, so we spent a very pleasant

time and were able to deliver bread and harvest loaves and plaits for the Thanksgiving.

Mrs D. Pounder

In Praise of Annie Hill

My foster mother was a real character of The Meadows. Her name was Annie Hill and she lived at No. 94 Briar Street. My mother gave me to her to look after. I always remember crying myself to sleep at night with tears for my mum. But she never came back.

Mrs Hill owned a wood-yard in Hawthorne Street where she and her husband chopped the wood and sold it. Also she would go in the very early

Kathleen outside No. 94 Briar Street in The Meadows.

Years later I ran away to join the ATS and wrote to Annie Hill. Evan, our next-door neighbour, read it to her because she couldn't read or write.

I came home on leave and it was then that I saw her, all 5ft nothing, with tears streaming down her cheeks. Suddenly I realized how much she had really loved me but she just didn't know how to show it. Years later when I had children of my own I began to call her Grandma. For the first time I called her anything but Annie Hill. She was lovely with my children and for the last four years of her life she came to live with me and my family.

Kathleen Kram

morning to the pit and load up her dray with coal and deliver it and fill her coal-house and then sell it from there. She would lift real heavy lumps of coal and weigh them, she really worked harder than any man and she was only about 5ft 2 inches tall.

One Bonfire Night her wood-yard caught fire where she had two horses and a dog, and she fought men to get through to save her beloved horse. In the end she succeeded. I am sure if it happened today she would have won a medal.

She loved animals almost more than people. She also used to smoke a clay pipe and wear a man's cap.

Kathleen Kram stationed in Germany, 1945.

Annie Hill never lost her love of horses, pictured in the twilight of her years.

A 'Mermaid' Came Calling

I lived in The Meadows on Woolmer Road and I have some great memories. Of Timpson's bakery, Mrs Jolliff's sweet shop and dancing at the St Faith's church hall on Saturday nights. Great bonfires in the street on the Fifth of November. Twopenny Talkies at Bridgeway Hall. Doing the washing at the old wash-house on Muskham Street. We also had Joan Stratford, who was the mermaid in the Trent Quincentenary Celebrations, staying with us while the shows were on. Someone came round knocking on doors to see if you could put someone up from the show near the Trent. Incidentally, I was married at St Faith's in 1958 and went to Trent Bridge Junior and Senior Girls' School.

Elizabeth Perkins (née Burton)

Doors Never Locked, Hearts Always Open

The Meadows was where I was raised as a child. They were the best years of my life. Every family that lived in Derwent Street were the finest families, every door in the street was always open, every person in the street was part and parcel, no ugliness. Mrs Carnelly was the midwife, although she had no formal training. Children were safe to play in the streets, and I remember when snow came up to the pantry windows, also the floods in 1947. I had got up to make a coal fire, and had to go down in the cellar for the coal. Before I got to the bottom step, I could see the water rising. I shouted to my mum and dad who were still upstairs in the bedroom, by the time they had come down, the water had risen to the top step of the

Dorothy Burton, mother of Elizabeth, pictured around 1957 in the back yard at Sutton Street which they shared with eight other premises.

Nottingham Forest football clubs. The club used to be run by Skip Mason. The top footballers were Ronnie Mann (Notts County), John Bailey (Forest), as well as the Jackson brothers who went to Notts County. Quite a few of us had trials with Notts boys.

All I can say is the area will never be the same as the old Meadows was, the attitude of people will never match the good old Meadows. The memories will never falter, the people of the old Meadows will never be matched, in hard times, in happiness, in friendship.

Fred Hart

cellar stairs. It gave us just enough time to get furniture up to the bedroom. It rose about 4ft in the living-room.

One thing you could rely on was the weather. When the winter came you knew that you would have snow, fog and very cold weather, then you could rely on the spring followed by the warmer weather of the summer. Each family used to collect old clothes, also rabbit skins, and take them to Tricket's down Trent Lane for cash. The money used to be saved up for a holiday to Skegness. Also, down The Meadows was Meadows Old Boys' Club, just beside the Trent Bridge Boys' and Girls' School, also Mundella School. The Meadows Boys' Club had a great football team with quite a few of the lads being picked by Notts County and

Rent spent, well not quite. Dorothy Burton's pink rent book for No. 43 Woolmer Road.

Meadows Old Boys Football Club, April 1955. Fred Hart is far right on the front row, his father, also Fred, is the gentleman in hat and coat on the back row.

Truly From the Cradle to the Grave

They called it the good old days of The Meadows, but some of it was not so good, as I so well recall.

We lived on Glapton Road, to be precise at No. 12 Conisbourgh Terrace. Off Glapton Road came six terraces named after different places, Attercliffe, Barnsley, Conisborough, Doncaster, Eckington and Ferriby. And each terrace had sixteen houses on each side, and each terrace had its own community and the twain never mixed, because Doncaster, Eckington and Ferriby thought they were a bit more upper class than the ones at the other end, because they were nearer the Embankment and River Trent than we were, and so life went on.

In the community you were looked after from the cradle to the grave by the people who did it best. Nobody fell out with each other and everyone respected their neighbour. Our dad and mother, George and Millicent Chambers, were strict but good parents. We had to go to Sunday school every Sunday with the Driscoll's family, Ellen, Dennis, Frances and Peggy.

There was the lady at No. 6, she had been a nurse in the 1914-1918 war. She was always on maternity call because the women at that time had their confinements at home because there was not all the modern technology of today. It was just a grunt and a groan, push and a squeeze, a smack on its bottom, the cry and the baby was born.

Next on the scene would be Mr Jacobs. He lived at the bottom house with his wife and family. He was a Jewish gentleman. If it was a boy, he would come round after five days and say to the mother, 'Would you like the boy to be circumcised, as it would be

51

beneficial in later life' in his Jewish accent. If you said yes, we never knew whether all the boys in the terrace were Jews or gentile, because when he came to perform this thing, he would do it on the front room table or on the piano keyboard with the lid down. He would come with his kit, cut-throat razor, candle in holder, a piece of wire made in a loop on a wooden handle. He wore his little Jewish cap on the back of his head and a white shawl round his shoulders. It took about ten minutes to perform, then he would say, 'Come and fetch the child Missus' when it was all over, for which he charged two shillings.

Everybody was christened in the church of their choice, and everybody came to the christening tea afterwards, even Mr and Mrs Jacobs, but we will never know whether he got in first and put you in the Jewish faith!

The lady at No. 22 was the expert if anybody was constipated or had a stoppage of the bowels. First of all she would send her daughter to the chemist for one pennyworth of liquorice powder. It was in a fold of paper so she would halve it and mix it in warm water and you had to drink it. Well, I can tell you it was horrible and, ask for a toffee afterwards – no chance! If that did not work, she would give you an enema, and this was a right performance. She would come with the tools of her trade, a length of rubber tube, a jug of warm soapy water, and a bakelite tube with holes in would be sterilized before it was used. It was then inserted in the back passage of the poor soul on the receiving end of all this, and if that did not move you, nothing would.

Then when anybody got married it was a big occasion. On the day of the wedding, all the girls of the bride's age would go to the house and assist in getting the bride ready. When it came time to go to the church, up came the horse and carriage (the only difference between a wedding and a funeral was the driver wore a white ribbon in his top hat, the horses wore white bows and white ribbon on the harness) and all the neighbours would line the pavement to see the bride off.

One other occasion was Bonfire Night, the Fifth of November. The youngsters would go round and collect all the rubbish they could find, and on the night would make a big bonfire in the middle of the terrace, and with fireworks, sparklers and bonfire toffee. Everyone had a good time till the early hours of the morning. The fire was so big, it melted the paint on the doors, but clearing up the mess next day was another matter for the dustbin men.

The last act would be Mrs Simmonds at No. 10. Whenever anyone passed on, off the terrace, it was her job to lay them out ready for the undertaker when he brought the coffin, and she was a comfort to those who were left. Once again, all the community would draw all the blinds of their windows, line the pavement and, in respect, see them off.

Eric Chambers

Mr Maltby and the Ticket to Ride

My husband's father Dennis Alvey was connected with the area, and the names of three of his brothers were inscribed on the memorial plaque on London Road School (First World War). For myself, I was born in 1914 and lived on Arkwright Street. I was married in St Saviour's church in 1945.

We know one brother was called Owen and we have been able to discover some of his wartime history on the internet. We would like to find the names of the other two brothers and hopefully trace their history. Unfortunately the plaque was removed when the school was demolished some years ago.

My father-in-law's family emigrated to Canada early in the century and some of the older boys returned to England.

My father-in-law remained in Canada and joined the Argyll and Sutherland Highlanders. He returned to England with his regiment during the First World War where he met and married my husband's mother, Rose Elizabeth Tomlinson.

During the Second World War, history repeated itself – my husband Harry visited relatives in Nottingham and that was how we met and were married.

I went to Trent Bridge School from the age of five, then I attended Nottingham Girls' High School, having won a scholarship.

I have fond memories of the teachers at Trent Bridge School. Miss Raistrick who fired our imaginations in various ways. She read from the newspaper each morning keeping us informed of the progress of the excavations at the Egyptian tombs and taking us on trips to nearby places of historical interest such as Standard Hill, East Bridgford and Mortimer's Hole at the castle. Miss Davey who grew hyacinths on her desk. Miss Jacobs who played the piano as we left the morning assembly. The music could vary from *Finlandia* to the *Peer Gynt Suite* and Miss Jacobs explained the music.

At Arkwright Street, we lived at No. 188, Stoake's shoe repair shop. We were just opposite the New Bridge Inn. The landlord was Sydney Tillingham. He was a cricket fan and many cricketers were his personal friends and visited the inn during the cricket season.

Mr and Mrs Dennis Alvey, pictured on their wedding day at Wilford church in 1918. History repeated itself during the Second World War when their son Harry met a Meadows girl, Caroline, and the couple were married at St Saviour's.

Nearby my home was Tongue's cake shop. The bread was made in the bakehouse behind the shop. You can imagine the delicious aroma that came from the bread – and then there were the queen-cakes.

There was also another shop whose proprietor was named Maltby. One of his daughters was a teacher at Trent Bridge School. He had a small sign which he used to put out daily. One side read: 'Ladies and gentlemen tonight to ride'. He meant bicycles of course but the sign, like Mr Maltby, was quite old and in later years it became a source of much amusement.

I recall huge turkeys hanging in a nearby fish shop at Christmas-time. We had a chicken Christmas Day, a rare treat in those days, and my mother's homemade Christmas pudding with custard. The pudding was made weeks previously and re-steamed on Christmas Day, for several hours.

Many of the side streets off Arkwright Street had shops. Orange Street for instance. There was Mudiman's, later it was Hooley's, they sold groceries and sweets. Luckett's, greengroceries, etc. Mrs Luckett bought direct from local market gardeners, in season. Langford's dairy. I went to Trent Bridge School with Phyllis Langford, she won a scholarship to Mundella School. Mr Langford had an ice-cream churn which he would use on a very hot day. We would wait outside the shop, coin in our hand, until the ice-cream was ready. There was also a newsagent and window-cleaning business.

A shopping trip in those days was like a social event, you could buy almost everything locally and you met people you knew. I don't think my mother would enjoy pushing a grocery cart round a supermarket the way she enjoyed her almost daily shopping trip.

Caroline Alvey

Moving Times but was it Progress?

During the 1960s I was a nurse in The Meadows, visiting homes and most of the schools. I set up and ran minor-ailment clinics in the Arkwright and Welbeck schools on three mornings a week. I walked from one to the other to see the many children who came to the clinics with various problems. The most common treatment was for the removal of verrucas. They often lasted for weeks and during that time children were excluded from swimming. Cut fingers, grazed knees, blocked ears and head lice were also treated. Children came for eye testing and hearing assessments; they were always friendly and usually wanted to stay and chat – perhaps the visit was a good excuse to leave their lessons!

Most of the families I visited were welcoming and friendly. Some mothers struggled to feed and clothe their families; they had low budgets as many of us had in the 1960s. I particularly remember the changes in Queen's Drive. The once stately homes, with carriage spaces behind the houses, became too large for one family. The houses were converted into flats and rooms; some had eight families living in one house. New residents arrived from different city areas and beyond; familiar families moved away.

The schools were staffed by very caring, dedicated staff. Mrs Brookes was headteacher at Arkwright Infant School. She spent time every morning hearing individual children read; she praised and encouraged them and they loved her! Mr Hutchinson was head of the junior school. Miss Mumby and Mr Howitt were heads at Welbeck Infant and Junior schools. The staff were always concerned for the children's welfare and gave them and their families help and support. Miss Lindley was headteacher at Brierley Nursery School and she and her staff gave wonderful guidance to the hundreds of little children who passed through. Miss Lindley was strict about timekeeping and locked the front door at 9 a.m. That was unfortunate for those who came late – they were usually on time the following day!

I remember visiting Trent Bridge Secondary Girls' School and meeting Miss Presley, the formidable headmistress. She expected and received high standards from her girls, both academically and in behaviour; sashes were awarded for deportment. When I visited for eye testing and for medicals, there were never any discipline problems! I've heard since that employers were glad to employ Trent Bridge girls as they were polite, dependable and good timekeepers.

In the middle and late 1960s, many families gradually moved to the new Clifton Estate. Those I met after the move had a few regrets; they missed the narrow streets, familiar neighbours, corner shops and the nearness of the city centre. It was then that I also left The Meadows area to work in Bulwell for a few years.

I remember the old Meadows with affection. Most of the children were lively and cheerful; they always spoke to me outside school – 'Ey up, nurse' was shouted across the streets and in the shops. I've met several of them since, now in their thirties with children of their own. I hope they also have happy memories of their 'Meadows days'.

Anne Moore

The grandeur of Queen's Drive, afforded by its impressively fronted and large Victorian houses, had faded by the 1960s. Many were converted into flats or bed and breakfast establishments as a generation moved out. By 1977, looking towards the Cremorne public house, it had all but gone. (photograph: H.L. Mercer)

Above: *The police station on the corner of Queen's Walk at Kirkewhite Street East, looking up Queen's Drive towards the LMS railway station in 1936. The route was also a victim of shifting priorities brought about by social change.* Below: *When uprooted to more spacious and greener locations such as the new Clifton Estate, to the south of the River Trent, former residents yearned for the narrow confines and close affinity with neighbours that was endemic in The Meadows in roads like Rupert Street pictured earmarked for demolition in 1976. (photograph: H.L. Mercer)*

Fish Jack and Trusting Lucy Ligo

Apart from military service – three years in the Royal Artillery before the war, and then war service – I have lived in The Meadows for almost all of the eighty-three years of my life. The Meadows I know and knew best stretches from Arkwright Street westward to what is now the Royal Ordnance complex but which began as a branch of Cammell Laird's of Birkenhead.

Having been born in 1916, I knew the 1920s well as a child. Our main street was Wilford Road, down which rattled and charged the No. 7 chocolate and cream tram which, being no buffers at the Embankment end, often overran the lines and we kids would help to push it back on again. It was said that one such tram once careered into the Trent; but that river being at a right angle to the lines, I never really believed that one.

Speaking of pushing, the old Cammell's works used to make rolling-stock for the Indian railways. Again, we kids helped push these great things from the works to an especially erected dock on the Trent side, prior to loading in barges for the journey, presumably to Hull.

Situated in Launder Street, cut through between Deering Street and the Kirkewhite Street end of Wilford Road, was what must have been the smallest school in all Nottingham. It was but one room with a bell-cote at its upper-front gable end which tolled the infant pupils to lessons just like any village school. You had to be 'well in' to have the privilege to ring that bell in the morning. I never made it.

The school had exactly a staff of three: the headmistress Miss Bowler (who also taught), Miss Adams, and Miss Chambers. Do you know – it was an infants' school with a separate infants' class; how infant can you get?

The teaching method was archaic to say the least. We would intone, 'a-te: AT; c-at: CAT; a-te: ATE; pl-ate: PLATE' and so on. Miss Bowler belonged to a long-gone age. We left that school at eight, to further our education at a more senior place. My departure year was 1924.

Things and characters stand out. There was Mr Hogg, the cobbler at the corner of Essex Street and Wilford Road. He proudly displayed to us the very first loudspeaker wireless in our neck of The Meadows, with its black horn wrenching out some 1920s song or other. There was 'Fish Jack', though not of The Meadows he would come trundling along our streets, calling out, 'Mackerel, congereelie, codfish, collie, plaice' while he chided tardy customers who had not paid their coppers which he allowed on tick. There were lots of eccentrics around, but two are worth noting: opposite each other at the Hawthorne Street end of Bosworth Road were the two shops of Lucy Ligo and Mrs Nightingale. Lucy was a trusting old soul, and you would ask for an empty box out of the back, and when her back was turned, greedy little hands would dive into a sweet-jar and, well, you know the rest. Mrs Nightingale opposite was a real character: stout, blowsy, dishevelled, her business methods were chaotic. She allowed tick (they all did), and she would use the torn-off bottom of a box of Woodbine fags to tot up the weekly 'own up'. There were so many of them, they would get 'lost', mixed up, trodden on and often rendered indecipherable. How that woman kept her sanity, I'll never know.

I well remember the Great Strike of 1926; we kids would stand outside of Jardine factory in Deering Street to watch the striking miners trying to 'urge' the men off their machines. The desire to come out was not universal.

Clifton Colliery was a source of employment for many working men in The Meadows. Its Miners Welfare still flourishes but the pit itself was closed in March 1969. Industrial units now stand on the site. The last three miners at the colliery, pictured on closing day, are, from left to right: Walter Smith, Ken Dudley and Brian Prince.

During the big depression, cinemas were hit badly; the old Imperial in Wilford Road hit back with a small bag of sweets per nipper admission.

The 'owd Meders' had something of a dubious reputation, I can't think why: we were a humble lot, very basic and perhaps a little stroppy here and there, but we didn't kick each other half to death, threaten each other with dire consequences and terrorize each other generally.

I'll finish up with a little self-spun parody of the old Scottish *Roamin' in the Gloamin'*.

I'm a-roamin' in The Meadows
On the bonny banks of Trent
I'm roamin' in The Meadows –
When all me cash is spent.
When the pubs have killed me thirst
And beer has done its worst
I'll be roamin', roamin', roamin'
in The Meadows.

E. Boddington

A Life in Harmony

In the early 1940s our family lived at No. 126 London Road and I attended London Road School where I played in the football and cricket teams. Later, I went on to train with Nottingham Forest FC in the days of Billy Walker. If anyone remembers me, I was a trainee motor mechanic at Oscroft's garage on Castle Boulevard and I played music for the Salvation Army by Victoria Market before eventually joining East Surrey Regiment in the regimental band.

Doug Caudrey

Our Foundry Father

My memories of The Meadows centre around my dad's foundry on Colliery Road. It was called Midco and was run by my dad, Tom Middleton, and his partners Cyril Middup and Ken Middleton (my uncle). I believe it

Celebration for Midco. Tom Middleton is on the far right, his brother Ken is third from the right.

NOAH'S ARK TO FACTORY

FEB 1947

Nottm. Fair Engines Kept Work Going

A generator which normally drives the Noah's Ark attraction at local fairs is at present enabling a Nottingham firm to maintain production on important work for the Government's Atomic Research Station at Didcot.

To-day a " Post " representative visited the factory of Messrs. Midco Steam Specialists, Ltd., of Colliery-road, Wilford Bridge, where 70 men have been kept out of the ranks of the unemployed by one of Messrs. Proctor's fair generators.

There it was stated that the firm would have closed down completely when the cuts were imposed last Monday, but by improvisation normal production had been maintained.

A report in the Nottingham Evening Post *during the 1947 floods revealed how a generator that powered fairground attractions such as Proctor's Noah's Ark ride, maintained production at Midco and thus helped sustain progress at the Atomic Research Station at Didcot.*

was founded about 1928 and was engulfed by larger concerns in the late 1960s. It was about where Wickes is now. They made mainly valves and pressure gauges of all sizes.

I can remember Bill Taylor and his wife who had a shop in one of the streets nearby but had a hut on the riverside of Colliery Road to serve the pedestrian traffic from Midco, Sturtivants and Clifton Pit. The Taylors had a son called Norman who played the xylophone.

There was Maisie who made the patterns for the castings – she had previously worked in a ladies' outfitters. Plus Enid, Lionel, Gordon, Joe, Billy, Bryn and many more. A colourful figure was that of Ivy who collected tolls on Wilford Bridge.

Miss M. Middleton

Faith's, Hope and Charity Too

Now aged seventy-six I was born on Hawthorne Street, No. 29, which was a confectionery shop right opposite the boys' entrance of the Bosworth School, which I attended until I was eleven, then on to the Senior Girls' of Queen's Walk. My brother had a coal business there, where they had stables at the back of our houses. We had several horses and ponies. The name of the business was Morley & Son, which is still going today run by my nephew.

My memories of The Meadows are very happy ones. I have been left there now nearly forty years, but we kept our connections with neighbours and friends. I was married at St Faith's church, which was our parish during the war.

The foundry jazz band at Midco.

I can remember three floods: 1932, 1945 and the big one of 1947. I had just moved into a small house on Hope Street in November 1946, then came the floods of the following March. They ruined everything as we were still on coupons and had dockets for furniture, lino, etc.

My husband was taken to hospital during the floods as he developed pneumonia, but he got over that okay and went on to start a football club called Ferry Rangers, which was organized in my home.

We had great fun and most people round The Meadows supported us. We held training sessions down the Embankment on a Sunday afternoon and took a portable gramophone for entertainment, it was real fun.

I moved from Hope Street to Bosworth Road in 1950.

I. Clarkstone-Priestley (née Morley)

Every Picture Tells a Story

More than anything, it was the folk of the old Meadows that made it such a happy place to live.

From school-days to working-days, I have fond memories of growing up, the area, and several photographs that record the changing faces of residents and show the sort of streets that were our homes.

Freda Mulvey (née Haslam)

Lifetime Links Maintained

Although I was not born in The Meadows area, throughout my life I have had an almost continuous association with the district. I was born close on Castle Boulevard, near to the Castle Rock, and from a very early age was taken by my parents through The Meadows to

The Ferry Rangers Football Club, team photograph taken around 1950.

Ivy Clarkstone, as she was then, with four members of Ferry Rangers, the team managed by her husband, on Briar Street following a Sunday training session on the Embankment.

The Bosworth Road School agility team, class of 1955.

Freda Mulvey pictured outside Astle's fruit and veg shop on Wilford Road in 1960.

return journey, it was always a treat to stop at a wooden structure known as the Hut, midway along Colliery Road, where we were able to purchase a hot or cold Vantas drink in a glass for the cost of one halfpenny.

I would often spend a whole day by myself at Fairham Brook at Wilford, fishing with a home-made rod, and return home carrying a can containing my catch.

At the age of eleven, I started at Mundella School and walked or ran the mile or so's journey four times daily. It never occurred to me to catch a bus or tram in those days. Our weekly games session of soccer or cricket was played on the fields adjacent to the school and most evenings I

the River Trent, this being the nearest place where it was possible to indulge in any ball game, fish for tiddlers or generally play without fear of injury.

As I grew older, I spent more of my time in the area, exploring different routes, until I was familiar with nearly every street and terrace. Very occasionally, my parents would take me for a river trip from Trent Bridge to Colwick Park, on one or other of the three steamers operating there. I believe they were named *Queen*, *Princess* and *Sunbeam*. The fare was sixpence and half-price for children.

When I was old enough, accompanied by one or more of my friends, we would make our way along Colliery Road to a field at the side of the power-station, in order to have an impromptu kick-about with a football, after walking a couple of miles to get there. On the

Catching up on the latest news around 1960 are, from left to right, Alan Mulvey, John Odell, Billy Kent and John Kent, suitably attired for the period on the corner of Hawthorne Street and Bosworth Road with the typical sort of Meadows terraced-houses in the background.

would again return to the fields to watch matches being played there or to play myself with anyone willing to join in.

After leaving school, I had a passion for running, and in order to train, dressed in a pair of shorts, I would wait until dark before venturing out to the Embankment, via the quickest route through The Meadows. Although a common sight nowadays, in pre-war days if I had been seen running through the streets in a pair of shorts, it would have attracted so much attention and I would have been labelled as being quite mad. Also for a short time I visited the Trent baths in the early morning for a quick dip, but gave up this practice after catching a few colds.

With the passing of time, my interests turned to the opposite sex, and I courted and subsequently married a girl who lived on Mundella Road. We had been to the school at the same time but I had never previously spoken to her until we again met working at the same place, for the Post Office Engineering Department, and we have now been together for almost sixty years.

During the early years of our marriage, the Embankment area was a favourite venue and we often took our young daughter to the newly constructed paddling pool, which was a great attraction for so many people with children.

My association with The Meadows did not end there, for I joined the Nottingham City Police, and worked consistently from Queen's Drive and Canal Street police stations for a number of years. Furthermore, following an early retirement on health grounds from the force, I joined the staff of the Prudential Assurance Company and worked for them as an agent in The Meadows for four years. I regularly called at many houses on Wilford Road, Traffic Street, Waterway Street, Kinglake Street,

Alan Mulvey, Brian Wood, and Ron Hurst pose outside the Clifton Miners Welfare, known locally as the 'stute, on Bosworth Road with the school in the background.

Middle Furlong Road, Rupert Street and Watt Street, together with all the numerous terraces, leading therefrom, collecting premiums, dealing with claims and paying out sick-benefits. National Insurance had not been introduced and cash benefits were paid out by Friendly Societies and insurance companies. Following promotion I was transferred to another district but much later in retirement we moved to a flat in sheltered housing accommodation in West Bridgford. From our nearby home, we often drive through The Meadows area, often getting lost, and now hardly recognising any of the old landmarks beside which we grew up, but I will never forget the greater part of my life spent in such a happy environment.

Harold E. Mettham

The Welfare was a thriving hub at the centre of the community, providing entertainment acts and a social focal point for residents. Recreation came in the form of darts, dominoes and long alley skittles. The 1962 B team celebrate winning their league.

A year later, a more formal team photograph records further success.

The Day the Earth Moved

During the 1950s I, along with my parents and brother and sister, lived in Blackstone Street in a block of houses owned by the railway.

Twice a day an express train came along the viaduct situated across the huge yard which ran at the back of our houses. At one end of the yard were the lavatories for each household and every family had its own key.

One night I was sitting opposite my mother, who was reading one of her green Penguin murder books in the kitchen-cum-living-room at the back of the house. Because of the shadow cast by the blue-bricked viaduct, the unshaded light was on for most of the day. The house shook but we didn't say anything, expecting a train to pass by in a few minutes, the train's

Mr Willars's mother standing by the outside lavatories with railway viaduct in background.

reverberations happening a long time before it drew level with the house. We looked at each other and my mother said, 'Has the train been by yet?' I replied in the negative.

The next day we learned that it had been an earth tremor. I think that it was 1957 and I believe that there was another tremor that year.

At the base of the viaduct there were spaces for storage, stables which were later used for cars, and workshops. At least one year the visiting circus from The Forest housed their animals under the viaduct and I certainly remember llamas and elephants being herded down 'Arky' towards the stables and being woken up one morning by the sound of an elephant trumpeting.

Michael Willars

Mr Willars's brother with bicycle on Blackstone Street in the late 1950s.

A Willars family outing in 1949, Michael with his sister and parents at the suspension bridge on the Victoria Embankment.

Underneath the Arches

In 1948 I started work at the small joinery/electrical firm of Curtiss Bros, Blackstone Street. The premises consisted of several arches under the railway viaduct.

One of the nicest characters was the father of the two Curtiss brothers. He was a delightful old man who enjoyed pottering about the joinery workshop in his working dress of boiler suit and bowler hat. My first job of the day started on the way to work. I had to queue at the kiosk outside the Midland Station for a packet of cigarettes (one packet per customer) for one of the senior joiners.

One of my jobs was to top-up an enormous black kettle which was kept on the boil on a gas ring throughout the day. Attached to the spout of the kettle was a length of rubber tubing which fed into a length of 12 inch diameter steel pipe. Inside the pipe was placed a long wooden spar which was to form the roof of the shooting brake. At the end of the day it was removed from the pipe and clamped onto a former where it was left to dry out. A Heath Robinson but effective process!

In those days a lot of pre-war cars were being converted into shooting brakes with wooden bodywork aft of the driver's cab. One job was to convert an old Rolls-Royce into a builder's pick-up truck.

The firm didn't have its own truck for delivering materials and I often had to push a loaded handcart through the city centre to various premises where work was in progress. Imagine this in today's traffic!

Brian Jones

Ivan Pearson with his two daughters Ann and Christine at the Pleasure Park or Beach, as it was alternatively known, at Colwick. The simple amusements and warm welcome extended by its owners proved a popular attraction to Meadows families, especially those with younger children. Having boarded a steamer at Trent Bridge, they had reached a destination within minutes where they would idle away entire days at the weekend and during holidays.

The Best of Times, the Worst of Times...

Although I originate from Radford, I married a Meadows girl and lived there for sixty-one years of my life. I found them very friendly and jovial people. I lived on Hawthorne Street, on one side of which was a wasteland known as the Hollows. When the Second World War broke out they decided to build an air-raid shelter of brick and concrete and the first time this came into real use was in May 1941. One bomb dropped on land near the Cremorne Hotel which was frequented by show and fairground folk. As a result, Mrs Proctor and her daughter Maisie were killed.

R. Woodward

Daily Dip in the Trent

My parents (Fred and Winnie Booth) had a beer-off at No. 178 Arkwright Street for forty-four years until their retirement in May 1974. I believe they were the longest-serving business in the area.

Amongst their souvenirs is a photo showing my father along with several friends at the old River Trent Baths, where they would visit most mornings all the year round. I remember as a very young girl taking hot mince pies to the swimmers on Christmas Day morning – my father taught me to swim as a five-year-old girl in the River Trent. On one of my visits the police were bringing a body out of the water.

Mrs Joan Stephens

69

Fred Booth, third from the right, and friends line up for a swim in the River Trent Baths, which were adjacent to the banks. Mr Pentecost of dyers Hicking & Pentecost, is on the extreme right. He would arrive for his bathing in a chauffeur-driven car. Water was an ever present danger to youngsters in The Meadows, some of whom discovered to their cost that the attractions of the rivers Trent and Leen and the Nottingham canal could be a fatal one.

The Clifton Hotel darts team, celebrating winning the Shipstone's darts challenge cup in 1959, pictured getting rather jolly at the Greyfriars Hall.

Shops and small businesses on Arkwright Street were severely hit by traffic and parking restrictions introduced by the city council in the 1970s. Gradually the life-blood was drained from the road and its doomed environs. Local business owners protested on the steps of the Guildhall with Tom Lynch of the National Union of Small Shopkeepers, fourth right, bottom row. Fred Booth is top left in the light-coloured coat while far right is Pat Murphy who had a shoe repair business a few doors up from Mr Booth's off-licence.

Workers pictured in the 1920s helping with the construction of Wilford Power Station, which stood adjacent to Clifton Colliery on the north bank of the River Trent. Dismantled two decades ago, industrial units and a fish and chip shop of the Harry Ramsden chain now stand in its place.

CHAPTER 3

Places

The railway bridge over Arkwright Street, a landmark in the region, pictured during the floods of 1947. The view is looking down the street from the Midland Station towards Trent Bridge. On the left, the billboard beneath the 'Player's Please' poster advertises events at the Queen's Cinema.

Railway Links

All the terraces were named after railways in The Meadows. In the 1930s the R100 airship passed over the area, being a marvellous sight in those days. My family and I then moved to No. 65 Woolmer Road. The building at the end of the yard used to be the old Eldorado ice-cream factory.

In 1937 we moved to a newsagent's shop in Kirkewhite Street known as Tarry's which was demolished in 1974. Bridgeway Hall was opposite which has now been rebuilt and the cross which stands now is made from two wooden beams from the old building. During the war years tea was served up the stairs and this was opened by the then Duke of Kent.

Another point of interest was that the Portland Baths in Muskham Street were covered on a Saturday morning to make a roller-skating rink.

There was a cinema opened at the junction of Mayfield Grove and Kirkewhite Street – the first film being *Sanders of the River* starring Paul Robeson. The other cinemas were the Queen's, the Grove and the Imperial. The schools were Collygate, Mundella, Trent Bridge Junior and Senior.

My grandfather was the foreman of the workers who put in the base of the suspension bridge. Whilst working on the base he was asked by a councillor to build ground for a small ferry over to Greshams and he was promised £5 for the job. He never was paid, so he put in a large white stone to remind him each time he used the ferry. As a child I always pointed this out to my pals. I do believe it is still there but was covered by the steps which were built to prevent flooding.

J.D. Tarry

Pulling Power of the Griffin

I was the landlord of the Griffin Inn on Waterway Street during the 1960s.

There were many good stories of different people who lived in this area.

One in particular was old Fats Stacey and his wife May. They were the local rag-and-bone man and wife who visited my pub regularly. They would come in most days of the week to sell good clothes for threepence, sixpence, or perhaps one shilling. He would tip them on the vault's floor at dinner time and the old girls would come in, have a drink and buy them. Sometimes they were very good clothes from The Park or Castle Boulevard.

I used to run a tote for the OAPs for Christmas as did most pubs as well as for the Ambulance Service at Beechdale Road. The draw was Sunday evenings at the Old Rose, Radford. With this, we took them on outings, also a sit-down meal at the Pavilion Hotel, Long Eaton near the motor bike track.

They were very good, poor days, not like today. They don't know how to enjoy themselves now, it's all money! money!

Ron and Clarice Whyler

Shake, Rattle and Roll in the Rain

As a group of young people we often visited a club on Wilford Crescent East run by two sisters, one named Dolly Alford, and an older man who was one of the sister's boyfriend. They later ran the Denman pub on Greyfriars Gate. The club was above an old garage and access to it was up some rickety wooden steps. It had a corrugated tin roof, which let the rain in and rattled. I never knew the name of it. The girl I went with to the club I eventually married – still together. I am now seventy-one.

Mr J. Porter

Watching the Trains Go By

My working life began at William Gibson's Hosiery Manufacturers at the corner of Arkwright Street and Cromford Street in April 1952. I was trained as a knitting-machine mechanic, my first pay-packet came to £1 12s $\frac{1}{2}$d for a 50 or 52 hour week, but they were happy days.

Our workshop was on the top floor and overlooked the platform of the Arkwright

Arkwright Street, 1959: a pivotal arterial route and thriving thoroughfare that played host to a huge variety of shops, public houses and characters.

Street station, so we could see the *Master Cutler* and others going to and from London. They always seemed to be full.

When the River Trent came up to flood levels, we used to have to go in and move the yarn out of the cellars before the water became too high in the lift-shaft wells, as the water came up through the ground. It was all built on water-meadows as the name suggests.

I used to cycle into work from West Bridgford but most of the people came from round The Meadows, and a better crowd of people would be hard to find. They may have been old houses, but most were kept like little palaces. Even in the 1950s there were traffic jams down Arkwright Street and London Road.

As a young lad, I was sent out on errands. Friday afternoon was to go to all the butchers' shops down Arkwright Street to buy chitterlings for the knitters on shift teas, and it was woe betide me if I didn't buy enough, or go out for the senior mechanics for boxes of snuff.

Sadly, like the old Meadows, the textiles are mostly finished.

Peter Phillips

Left: *Frederick and Winifred Booth, who celebrated 45 years at their off-licence at No. 178 Arkwright Street in 1975. Above: the shop interior with Mr and Mrs Booth at the counter.*

Shoppers' Paradise

Arkwright Street – shopping centre of The Meadows. There were nearly as many shops on Arkwright Street as there were in the city centre, you could do all your shopping without moving out of the street.

My mother worked at a firm called Baldwin's (head office of Bunny Brickworks), my father also worked there as a mechanic. Baldwin's directors also belonged to Notts County Football Club (it was they who brought Tommy Lawton to the club, he worked as a rep' for Baldwin's – his name mostly).

Another memory of Arkwright Street was when the Queen came to the city. On her way to the Victoria Embankment, the procession had to go down Arkwright Street from the Midland Station, and like the hundreds of people either side of the street, me and my family were there cheering. As the cars came nearer, the whole crowd moved forward knocking me off balance. Putting my hands out, I touched the royal car – a smile from Her Majesty and a helping arm from a nearby policeman, I was safely back on the pavement.

Another memory of the street was where all my pocket-money used to go, for it had enough toy and sweet shops to satisfy any child with money in their pockets.

Floods! Oh those floods near Trent Bridge and another way for children to make a shilling or two. We used to wade into the shallow parts asking the shops underwater if they needed any help, moving stock or trying to shovel water up with a dustpan and bucket. Another memory is trying to ride our bike in the deepest part to see if we could get our wheels to turn. That is until the police chased us off.

D.R. Glover

Happy Days Opposite Stevo's

When, as an eleven-year-old in 1945, our family moved to Waterway Street (London Road end) sandwiched between Pinders-House Road and Mabel Street, I did my schooling, firstly at London Road, then moved on to Trent Bridge where you found yourself categorized as a 'big boy'.

Mind you, academia wasn't at all my forte, so let sleeping dogs lie. I seem to have quite a retentive memory concerning my adolescence, I recall all our neighbours seemed to be happy folk. Horses and drays were to be seen most days plying their trade as it were. Often I would find the odd carrot or perhaps a slice of bread, and feed some lucky animal. We lived directly facing a huge warehouse known to all and sundry as Stevo's. Stevenson's in the main stored sugar in its large confines. Daily, vehicles would arrive and off-load innumerable sacks of sugar there. I often wonder with present day buildings in mind, what HRH Prince Charles would have made of it, a word springs to mind – 'carbuncle'.

We had ten shops on Waterway Street (in between London Road and Arkwright Street), mostly general stores, but we had a pork-butcher (Holliday's), plus the obligatory fish and chip shop (West's). Other shopkeepers on our street were namely, Wright's, Rudkin, Reast, Lloyd, Pottinger, Trigg, Green and Jones. Arkwright Street from the Midland Station to the Trent Bridge Embankment was literally a veritable hive of shops. You could purchase almost anything, from wet fish to wellingtons, faggots to furniture. It seemed all tastes were catered for. Whilst on the subject of food, it would be an absolute crime not to mention Hilda's, the fish and chip shop with the supper room situated on Kirkewhite Street. Her fish cakes were a gastronomic delight. After going to a local cinema in an evening, automatically I would visit her shop to buy her wares for my supper. We could choose from four cinemas in The Meadows, namely the Queen's, the Globe, the Grove and the Imperial. These four establishments were always a joy to visit, that is if you didn't mind queuing. Cinema-going was quite a popular pastime, it was literally an education for me. It taught me far more than school ever did.

Red ochre doorsteps and window-sills were the norm in those days. Occupants in each and every household took pride in helping to keep the street looking neat and tidy. My adolescent years were quite happy. One of the biggest 'social events' of the year was the Fifth of November. The obligatory bonfire on a piece of waste ground on Crocus Street, known as the Leeny to all the locals. That piece of ground was mostly tenanted by the Leeny Gang. In winter it became a football stadium, and in the summer cricket held sway. Local residents used to watch our juvenile antics for hours on end.

All in all, I'm sure all of my friends enjoyed every moment, money was scarce but happiness was abundant. It certainly doesn't look or seem the same to me when the bus taking me to town goes through the new Meadows. It's a thing called progress I'm readily reminded by fellow-travellers. I lived there almost forty years, I feel privileged at having done so. For sheer escapism I'll call it Walton's Mountain, and I'll pretend I'm John-Boy writing in his journal 'Goodnight everybody'.

David Robert Screen

Bathroom was a Rare Luxury

My father emigrated to Australia, where I was born but sadly my mother died and we came back to England. We lived with my grandparents at No. 148 Arkwright Street, the beer-off. I think the Booth's must have bought the shop from them – Mr and Mrs Burton. It was about 1921 when we first lived there. I don't think there was any bottled beer in those days, just draught. People came into the shop with their jugs for half a pint or a pint and they sold tobacco too.

I was always fascinated with the thick-twist, which looked like large rolls of liquorice. It was cut and weighed on small brass scales as little as half an ounce at a time. Between the beer-off and the shop next door (either the Meadow Dairy or the Maypole) there was a large cobbled alley, at the bottom of which were workshops. I can also recall hearing the pigs squeal as they were being slaughtered nearby.

My father married again, and we moved to the grocer's shop next door. The accommodation was at the back and over the top of the shop. We had a bathroom, which was very rare in those days. Towards town there was a large shop, which I believe sold motor cycles and accessories. The name was Houlton. Also in that block was a small shop which made pikelets and close to the beer-off stood a butcher's shop named Smeeton's. With great pleasure I always remember that further down Bunbury Street there was situated a small dairy where ice-cream was made. As children we loved to watch this process as a large tub full of ice-cream was placed in a hand-operated churn. Such happy days.

Mrs M. Mills

The Heart and Soul has Gone

From 1958 to 1975 we lived in The Meadows and those years were very happy ones. We moved three times but stayed in the region as the people were so nice, some of our best friends were all ones we met while living there.

Arkwright Street was a wonderful place to shop. I can't think of anything you

Above: *Annesley Street in 1971.* (*photograph: Geoffrey Oldfield*) Below: *The Toll Bridge end of Wilford Road taken five years later.* (*photograph: H.L. Mercer*)

Above: *Bunbury Street in all its glory.* Below: *Bunbury Street laid low by the bulldozers in 1971, on the junction with Orange Street.* (photographs: Geoffrey Oldfield)

couldn't get. Food and furniture shops, banks, churches, pubs, clothes and fishing-tackle, even pawnshops. Apart from the large stores, no one needed to go to town for anything. The Embankment was much nicer too, we could take the children to feed the swans, watch people in the rowing-boats for hire or go for a ride on the boats that ran up and down the river. The Memorial Gardens were beautiful with a lovely fishpond. My friends and I would spend nearly all day down by the river and the paddling pool with the kids during the school holidays.

When the slum clearance started and it all changed, The Meadows was never the same. The council did us no favours when they changed it all. I still visit friends who live in the new Meadows, but it is not the place it used to be. The heart seems to have been ripped out of it.

Mrs J. Gutteridge

Doors Were Never Locked

My early childhood was spent in The Meadows. I look back to that time with very, very happy memories. The people were the salt of the earth and would do anything to help out a neighbour with problems. Doors were not locked – the community spirit was high.

The Meadows enjoyed a variety of shops, especially in Arkwright Street. No need to go into the town centre – everything to hand. Grocers, fresh fish, butchers, paint/wallpaper, confectionery, dressmakers, shoe shops, pawnbrokers, etc.

My best recollections are skating for shopping the length and breadth of Arkwright Street and, oh yes, we even had a music shop selling all kinds of instruments, especially accordions, as well as some excellent mouthwatering sweet shops which kept us glued to the windows when pocket-money was received. Two confectioners shops were of special interest to me, with their enticing display of luscious cream cakes.

We could catch a boat to the Pleasure Park for the day, or listen to the band concerts held on the Embankment. A spot of fishing with our jam jars on string was another attraction. The Portland Baths opened their doors in winter to skaters, a false floor being put over the pool. In summer, we could swim there for a copper or two.

Bridgeway Hall was our Sunday school, attendance twice a day and the yearly Anniversary where we sang solos and recited passages was always looked forward to with delight. This came soon after Easter and we always had our new Sunday clothes bought for the Anniversary, often made by the dressmaker on Arkwright Street.

You could see some folks taking their jugs for liquid refreshment to the street corner off-licences.

Our local library was also a real special place, with its rows and rows of books of all kinds. I loved all the *William* books, and books on crime.

The Wall's ice-cream tricycle plied its trade at the school gates. If we were not too flush, we could buy half of a 'sucker' in something similar to a Toblerone wrapper.

Mrs J.P. Lloyd

Cobble-stone and Skipping Ropes

I was born in 1905, making me aged ninety-four on St George's Day, 23 April. It gives me great pleasure to write about the old days growing up in The Meadows, which I understand was called the Crocus Fields before the builders went in.

I was born in a house in Brand Street, which was chosen as a location for the film *The Ragman's Daughter* because of the cobble-stone road, about four doors away from my grandma and grandad (a policeman who was called Bobby Wheatley). Both my grandmas had eight children so I was never short of relations.

After school, I used to play games with my friends. Skipping was the favourite. A long rope was held, by a girl at each end, and we would jump in singing 'All in together girls, this fine weather girls'. Another game was 'lurky', which involved hiding in the entries of houses until we were found.

The streets near where we lived all led down to the River Trent, Freeth Street being along the bottom. My dad often went for a swim with his brothers. Along the top, on Meadow Lane, were Mrs Demelos's fish and chip shop and a butcher's. On the corner of Grainger Street there was Cooper's sweet shop. They made their own ice-cream which was lovely. I used to spend my Saturday's penny there to buy what I called 'a big plain one', a square of plain chocolate. My dad used to work at Taylor's factory. I always met him on pay-day for my penny.

The next street was Home Street with Truswell's beer-off on the corner. Then there was Meadow Grove leading to the tripe factory, and Mr Hall's bone works. We used to call it Bony Halls. When the bones were boiling for the glue, there was a nasty smell floating around.

Notts County played a prominent part in my life. Some of my friends married players such as Plaits, Cope, Death and Macpherson. Mabel, one friend, married Cope. Her parents kept a fruit and vegetable stall opposite Griffin & Spalding.

Mrs Kathleen Oakland

Soaking Up the Nostalgia

Until I was married in 1953, I lived in the old Meadows from 1933. Dad, Mam, sister Joan, brother Dennis and myself, Connie Smith. We all lived at No. 27 Briar Street, no inside toilet, no bathroom, just a large tin bath. The hot water came from a coal fire (plus anything else that would burn) copper in the small scullery which kept us cosy and warm, both in or out of the bath. Joan first, then me, and Dennis last. When we were older, we used the public baths in Hawthorne Street, an old twopence bought hot water, soap and use of a towel and the attendant cleaned the bath. We all went to Bosworth Road School from aged five to eleven. Joan and myself then went to Queen's Walk Girls' School, Dennis to Trent Bridge School. We had no worry about transport, we walked to school, then back home for dinner and walk again for the afternoon, no school meals or even a room to eat sandwiches.

When shopping, you went on Wilford Road, a good selection of shops for your every need. There was the Co-op with separate departments for grocery, bread and greengrocery, the pawnshop, Widdowson's chemists, Combe's shoe repairs. Toulson's pork-butchers, Frank Price fresh fish, Battersby's, Marsden's, Home and Colonial and many paper and tobacco shops. As children we were never bored. A walk up the street to the Embankment or the old halfpenny Toll Bridge end, always finding things to do. If frosty or snow, sledge and slides down the slopes or

Meadow Lane in the 1960s and Notts County's football ground to the left. The houses of Meadows residents backed up to a wall next to the old wooden main stand and concrete area where the players frequently staged five-a-side games. Balls kicked over the wall in the backyards of the houses were retrieved by apprentices asking something along the lines of: 'Could we have our ball back, please Mister'. More often than not it was returned by the occupants, who like the vast majority of the Meadows folk were County supporters. (photograph: Nottingham Evening Post)

break the ice on the paddling pool to see who could get the largest piece of ice. In summer, it was the paddling pool, playing rounders or ball games, fishing in the Trent with jam jars on string. If we stayed in the street, we would all skip, with an old piece of clothes-line stretched across Briar Street, with the other kids, named Joyce, Etches, Annie Smith, Jean Stevens, Maisie Oliver, Pat Yates, Barbara Hill, Peggy Walters and Gladys Smith.

Maybe we played 'tin lurky', hopscotch, jumping higher and higher, hide-and-seek for a change. On the Fifth of November we had a big bonfire in the middle of the road, loads to burn, most of it old furniture, not many fireworks, no one could afford them. A child's bag of chips cost one penny from Clara Parr's chip shop on Briar Street. Where Briar Street joined King's Meadow Road, stood the Salvation Army building where, throughout the winter for one night a week, they held a magic lantern show which cost a halfpenny.

I left school at fourteen and went to work at the Cellular Clothing Company in Traffic

A pint awaited on every corner in The Meadows. The Locomotive Inn, Wilford Road (above), the Poets Corner and the Rifleman Inn (opposite), both on Kirkewhite Street, were just three of the more famous, or in some cases infamous, watering-holes that quenched the thirst of the neighbourhood. (photographs: Nottingham Evening Post)

Street, walking to work and back. When the war started, they built communal air-raid shelters on our side of the street. On the opposite side, the even numbers, each house had its own brick shelter built in the back garden. Dad worked at the ROF gun factory. They drove tanks down King's Meadow Road to the factory, the vibrations shook the road, pavements and all the houses around. Mum worked at Jardine's factory in Deering Street. On the pavements in Queen's Walk and Queen's Drive were smoke-screens which they lit up at tea-time. The thick smoke and smell was awful, pollution now was nothing compared to being near them.

They were mostly happy times, without much money, but happy families, good neighbours and everyone helping one another. My mum stayed in the old house until rehoused in a flat in Lammas Gardens, still wishing to stay in The Meadows, hoping to keep near her old friends.

Connie Bemrose (née Smith)

Monday Night's Cattle Drive

I well remember The Meadows area in the early 1930s, not much money about, but plenty of laughter. For instance, every

Monday night cattle-drovers used to drive animals from the railway sidings at the bottom of Ryland Crescent, where they were unloaded from the cattle trucks, and driven through the streets, namely Wilford Grove, Wilford Crescent East, Woodward Street and on to and over Trent Bridge, and so eventually to Loughborough Road. We had small shops on most street corners, also the post office on Wilford Crescent East, managed by the parents of Leslie Crowther, the comedian. There was a wash-house on Bunbury Street and swimming and slipper baths, namely the Portland ones. Each night and morning a lamplighter would light or extinguish the street gas lamps. Us kids, as we were called in those days, could play happily on the streets, no fear of being run over, only by horse and carts, and we could hear them coming in plenty of time.

C.V. Parnham

The Cremorne Hotel

I wish to contribute a poem highlighting the times Dad and I spent the summer days together, visiting the Cremorne pub near the old Toll Bridge. They were happy days for us. We still think if those times together.

Across from Wilford Halfpenny Bridge
Stands the old Cremorne Hotel
Frequented by Dad and I
Many stories, we could tell
Dad and I together be
Out and about, go for a pint
We'd end up at the Cremorne
The landlord, usually kind
We would buy a round or two
Sit outside, take in the sun
Just watching the world go by

Yes it was, great mighty fun
Then decisions to be made
Would we walk, or would we bus
Usually we'd walk on home
Talking, walking, with no fuss
Count our pennies to the last
Even down to last half-pint
Looking back they were great days
To find today, is hard to find
To the Cremorne in The Meadows
Thank you for our happy days
Dad and I think of it now
Always will, come what may.

Anon

Awakened by the 'Caller-Up'

Though I was born a Lincolnian (with Meadows great-grandparents!), I spent all of my school-days in The Meadows, living first in Blackstone Street and then Glapton Road. I always considered Glapton Road as The Meadows. It is quite amazing how many of the city's councillors and aldermen came from that area, though I wonder did they admit it. I was once interviewed (unsuccessfully!) for a job by an alderman from the other end of the city and he took me to task for giving my address as The Meadows. He said all his acquaintances on that road called it Trent Bridge.

In the early 1930s, we had no wireless and our only form of 'canned' entertainment was a wind-up gramophone. I soon learned all the comedy records, chiefly Sandy Powell, by heart. Imagine our delight, when he came to play in a charity cricket match on the Queen's Hall recreation ground, known as 'the Cricket'. Was he the first comedian to use a catch phrase? I can remember we all chorused, 'Can you hear me mother!'

A place to watch the world go by: the Cremorne Hotel. Proctor's fair, fondly remembered by a generation, is no longer. (photograph: H.L. Mercer)

The 'Meadows at war' was a very sinister place, no one seems to remember the smoke-screens, horrible little stoves belching choking black smoke, particularly along Queen's Drive. The smoke was supposed to hide the city from view, then someone decided to put a huge searchlight on the Castle green, and it lit us up like daylight.

To us, the centre of the universe was Arkwright Street, with Wilford Road coming a close second!

Some people insisted it was Clapton Road as the 'G' on the road sign was not very clear. The houses were mainly, if not entirely, railway built. Those on the west side, and the terraces, were Great Central – later LNER. The terraces were alphabetically named after GC stations from Attercliffe through to Ferriby, so Glapton made sense. The houses on the east side were Midland Railway built. When we moved there in 1937, only four were still owned by the LMS. They were easily recognized to railway enthusiasts, as the front doors were painted the same colour as the famous Midland Compound locomotive. As an old Mundellan, I called the colour 'maroon'. One of my younger cousins, a railway enthusiast and photographer (later with *Lincolnshire Echo*), thought our house was ideally situated for seeing and photographing trains, as such prestigious trains as the *Master Cutler* passed over the nearby bridge over the river (and made the ornaments on the mantelpiece rattle!).

The Meadows had its own little fair at times during the year known as 'the Cremorne Wakes' as it was held on the land at the side of the Cremorne Hotel on Queen's Drive near Wilford Bridge. We used to visit the fair as youngsters. Unfortunately, on the night after the Nottingham Blitz a plane dropped a stack of bombs, one of which hit the laundry at Wilford Bridge, and caused fatalities among the fair folk who had left the air-raid shelter. Everyone studied the craters next day – did one bomb fall in the Trent? The target had obviously been the LNER railway bridge. The bombs also missed the Wilford Toll Bridge. We had to pay halfpenny each way to walk across the bridge, or for one penny as many times as we wished for a whole day. Sometimes, it was possible to crawl on all fours, and not be seen by the gatehouse keeper.

My father was on the railway and he was required to live within about a mile of the locomotive depot on Middle Furlong Road. If his shift time was altered during the night, the 'caller-up' came and knocked on the front wall of the terraced house. Father or mother would open the sash-window and answer. During the war, the message was usually 'on at once'. I often wonder what neighbours these days would think to a caller-up. In those days no one gave a second thought. Railwaymen had caller-ups and that was accepted in the same way the paper-sellers shouted 'Post sevny clock' as he delivered and tried to sell the late edition of the Evening Post.

I wrote a poem about Arkwright Street for a former Sheriff of Nottingham on his diamond wedding. At that time, The Meadows was not fully rebuilt – now I've had to change the last few lines:

Wot's appen'd to Arky

'Ah ya goin' on Arky?'
As kids we used to shout
'Ah ya goin' on Arky?
Mam not ya tek no out?'
You could buy owt on Arky
From hat-pins to big cars
From foreign stamps to three-piece suites
And 'apenny candy bars.

Scarrott's, Marden's. Goodchild's, Book's
Whitley's, Maypole, Simpkin's, Hames,
Bellamy's, Groves and Andy Bone
Just some familiar names.
At least two hundred places
Supplied the families' needs
With churches, pubs and pictures
A first-rate street indeed!

Posh folk came down Arky
To sing at Bridgeway Hall
And Magpies, Redo and Cricketers
And kids with bat and ball.
We saw the queues on Arky
For bread and cakes and sweets
For jars of jam and biscuits
And Whitley's high-class meats.

All through the war on Arky
The shops did their best
Supplied the food and clothing
To keep us fed and dressed.
The planners came to Arky
With their 'New Meadows Plan'
They closed it to through traffic
The troubles then began.

The Saint Saviour's Guides pictured in 1955. Janet Ball is second from the right in the back row.

The shops couldn't make a profit
No matter how they tried
No cars could get down Arky
In fact the whole street died.
The builders rebuilt Arky
Let's hope now they have done
The kids who live round Arky
Can still have lots of fun.

Mary E. Reed (née Martison, or to
Mundellans 'Martoc')

Saints Alive

I am writing to say how delighted I was to read about The Meadows in the April issue of *Bygones*. It brought back so many happy memories of my childhood there at Trent Bridge School and especially my time spent at St Saviour's church on Arkwright Street.

In recent years some of the former church members have met and been reunited through the valiant efforts of our former Guide captain from the 1950s, Margaret Mitchell (now Mrs Harris). At that time she was the daughter of the Revd Mitchell, the vicar of St Saviour's. From the initial reunion meeting some years ago, when six former church members met together, it has grown steadily to around forty. Its numbers included former choir members, youth club members and Guides.

When I attended St Saviour's in 1952, and onwards, there were a host of activities for the local young people to participate in throughout the week and especially on Sundays. We would give a warm welcome to any other past members from the 1950s when we hold our annual picnic on the Trent Embankment, usually during August, which provides an excellent opportunity for old friendships to be rekindled.

Mrs Janet Westcott (née Ball)

The Meadow Garage, owned by Mr Perrons, on Briar Street. (photograph: Michael Gardner)

The Meadows of Old

A dear friend of ours wrote this poem, and it seems appropriate. My wife was born down The Meadows in 1934 and remembers those days well.

T. Parkes

Do you remember The Meadows?
Those good old days
Where we played games round the streets
and alleyways?
Do you remember the Magna, the Loco
and the Castle?
Where you could sit and drink
without any hassle
We had the Vic pub and
Simmon's pot shop
And two pawnshops where you
pop in and pop

There was Toulson's pork shop and
Battersby's shoe shop
Home and Colonial, Plunket's the tailors
and the tripe shop

Go to Turner's fish shop for a
penn'orth of mixed
Then to the Imperial to watch the flicks
Or even the Grove, the Plaza
and the Queen's
Also the Globe to see stars on the screens
We had the Cremorne pub and
Proctor's fairground
For a penny a ride you could go
round and round.
Bosworth Road School, Queen's Walk and
Trent Bridge
In those days you were rich if you
owned a fridge

We would play hopscotch, 'ticky dob'
and rounders

Whip and top, hide-and-seek, and on the
Rec' you'd find us
As for television we'd never heard
of the word
Radios with accumulators that's
what we heard
St George's church and the Meadows hall
Those trep'ny hops where we
all had a ball
There was no discos or hi-fis for us
We made our own fun without all that fuss.

We had the beautiful Embankment to stroll

summer nights
To watch cricket or bowls or just
take in the sights
They took away our cinemas, our pubs
and our groves
Demolished our streets, our terraces,
our homes
But they can't take away our
memories we hold
Of the wonderful Meadows,
The Meadows of old

A.P. Buckross

The Welbeck School, formerly Queen's Walk, and the corner known as 'the Cricket'.

Festive Trunk-Call

When the trains went over Derwent Street, where I was born, the house would shake. I remember the night an elephant escaped from the stables on the street, everybody was woken up with the elephant dragging chains down the street. The papers said it was the 'fight of the two trunks'. It put its head through Arthur Linley's front door. Arthur ran downstairs with nothing on – thus the fight of the two trunks. It was on Christmas Eve, can't remember what year. It also pushed a car called *Genevieve* down the street onto Kirkewhite Street. The paper also said it was like seeing pink elephants. When the trainer arrived he shouted 'Baby'. The elephant put his trunk into the trainer's arm and went back to the stables like a baby.

I remember Bridgeway Hall Tuppenny Talkies for children of all ages under ninety-nine. All are welcome. A man who was in charge was always asleep at the back. We named him 'Sleeping Charlie'. I was also a member of the Meadows Boys' Club, a wonderful place with Skip Mason in charge. We recently held a reunion with many of us in our seventies. We had a group photo taken and then we broke out into The Meadows' war-chant: 'Boomeraka, boomeraka, who are we? We are the boys of the MBC. First in the war, first in the peace, first in the hands of the Nottingham police. M-E-A-D-O-W-S. Meadows!'

Before I finish I would like to mention Pete Richards, who scored 148 goals in one season playing for Clifton Miners Welfare in the Notts Amateur League. This proud record will never be beaten. Also the club on Wilford Crescent was called the Crescent. What happy memories.

Mr M. Hart

Mystery of the Hosene

Memories of childhood in The Meadows
I often recall
Football and cricket matches on
the tar pitch
Gudgeon snatching down roach hole
on the wall
All the things we kids did and the
old places we'd been
But nobody would ever tell me what they
made at the Hosene.

Saturday mornings running errands along
busy Wilford Road
Cycling back down Essex Street
with a heavy load
I remember King's Meadow Road and
Goodhead Street
They're the places where Pete the Cop
used to walk his beat
In telling lots of tales he was very keen
But even he wouldn't tell us what they
made at the Hosene.

Playing over the Tips, making fires
in the hollow
Riding down Pad to the train bridge where
Tony Rags the stray dog would follow
Coming home filthy, Mam saying
'Where have you been?'
But nobody would say what they
made at Hosene.

Then there was Clara's chip shop round
on Briar Street
Saturday afternoons at the Imperial
where at Christmas
You got an orange for a treat
Sunday was for Sunday school
at Sally's Army or
The chapel on King's Meadow Road
Winter evenings there was

Bosworth Play Centre
Somewhere to go out of the 'code'
A Friday trip to the baths on
Hawthorne Street
Made sure you were clean
But just what did they
make at the Hosene?

As you got a little older you went down
to the Santa Fay
A few underage jars in the Crescent or
The Sherbrook to help you on your way
This would be about the time I was fifteen
I still didn't know what they
made at the Hosene.

It's now many years since The Meadows
I left
But now I'm back down there working
Back on the old scene
And if I'm really honest
I think I did know what they
made at the Hosene.

Carl Enever

Smog-Bound From the River

I once lived on Harry Terrace, off Crocus Street, with my mother and father, Gwendoline and Frederick Barnett but I left the area when I was ten years old. I remember the smog which was particularly bad down The Meadows due to the proximity of the River Trent.

Crocus Street had three terraces, Harry, Mary and Ernest Terrace. There was a shop on the corner of Mary Terrace where I could buy two blackjack sweets for halfpenny.

I remember bath nights consisted of a zinc bath put in the kitchen on the cold stone floor and filled with hot water from the copper boiler. The toilet was outside, had a gap at the bottom of the door, and was very cold in winter. There was a train station on Arkwright Street just around the corner from Crocus Street. The station was on the bridge crossing Arkwright Street.

Graham Barnett

Traffic Congestion Breaks into a Trot

All roads led to Traffic Street, where I was born in 1923. At fourteen my sister and I worked at Derbyshire sweet factory in the street while four other sisters, a brother-in-law and my boyfriend worked at the Cellular Clothing Factory in the same road. To cap it all, my dad, two brothers and a brother-in-law worked at Frank Furnnis Bros, the abattoir (pigs) in Traffic Street. Now and again, a few pigs would run in our front door and out of the back with men chasing after them. Christmas was a very busy time, the men worked all night in the abattoir but my mother kept them going in tea and home-made cheese and bacon cobs.

I attended Queen's Walk School and was married at St George's church in The Meadows in 1945. On Saturday nights, we'd go dancing in the church hall. Without a bathroom we were forced to bathe at the Portland Baths, a soap and towel provided for fourpence. Mum and dad drank at the Queen's Hotel. Now our son Geoff takes us there. I go inside now but before I sat outside on the doorstep. As a small boy Geoff watched the trains go by Wilford Road. Now he drives them.

When we came home from school we had to fetch coal in a three-wheel barrow from Blackstone Street. They were very heavy,

Above and facing page: *Like most of Wilford Road, the pubs that lined its route are gone but not forgotten: among them were the Castle Inn, the Magna Carta and Locomotive Inn. (photographs: H.L. Mercer)*

but we got a cup of tea, bread and lard afterwards (well worth it).

Happy days. Wonderful memories.

Mrs Gladys Crowder

Cottage Industry

I was born in Lamcote Street in 1917 and later my parents had a shop at the bottom of the street. It sold sweets and grocery. My grandparents lived in Bunbury Street and I also had aunts and uncles in other streets. I went to London Road School and we also

had a shop on Crocus Street.

After that my parents gave up the shops and went to live in Norfolk Cottage which is still there at the back of the pub which was called the Norfolk Hotel on London Road. To get to our door we had to go up a slope in Dank's Yard which had stables wherein horses were kept. Our surname was Rose and my dad was quite well-known as he was a good pianist and singer and played at most of the pubs in The Meadows such as the Franklin, Poet's Corner, Norfolk Hotel and many others I can't recall.

Mrs Taylor

Mundella School pictured in its 50th anniversary year in 1947.

No Hot Water But What More Could Man (or Woman) Desire?

What a wonderful place to grow up. Both the city's football clubs and the cricket ground within walking distance, plus the River Trent and the Embankment. Four cinemas, the Queen's, the Globe, the Grove and the Imperial and a trolleybus service to Bulwell via the city every few minutes.

Horses for the railway delivery carts were stabled under the railway arches in Blackstone Street. Hanging from the back of the carts was a favourite pastime until you were spotted by the driver. Also under the railway arches in Cromford Street was a Lyons Tea warehouse where it was possible to earn a copper or two helping the salesmen to load the vans from trolleys – before going to school in the morning.

There were the local cricket 'test' matches between north, south, east and west, mostly taking place on the Embankment and the Queen's Drive cricket fields. They attracted large crowds.

In Traffic Street there was an abattoir from where an occasional unfortunate beast would escape causing a bit of excitement.

The area was well provided by secondary schools and Mundella Grammar School – what a crime it was ever pulled down. The Meadows Boys' Club, was built

One of two date stones, all that now remain of Mundella School.

by local solicitor R.J. Willatt in 1926 originally as a Boys' Brigade Club with some considerable foresight, including a large gymnasium which was used for many years by Trent Bridge School. Thousands of teenagers spent five or six nights a week at the club during the 1940s, 1950s and 1960s. The club held a high reputation in the National Association of Boys' Clubs of that era.

The Wilford Grove, Wilford Crescent, Beauvale Road, Bathley Street area is still recognisable but so much has changed. I lived in The Meadows area from the mid-1930s until 1952, housing was poor, no bathroom, no hot water and outside toilets, but we had never known anything else.

H.R. Hackland

Global Warning

I was projectionist at the Globe Cinema, near Trent Bridge in 1942. It was a continuous performance from 2 p.m. to 11 p.m., there being no Sunday cinemas during the war years. We had a slide to impose over the film that warned patrons that air-raid sirens had sounded and that for those patrons wishing to remain 'the show will go on.'

Many people will remember Tom's Café at the London Road side of the cinema. Tea was twopence a cup. Some of the films remembered are *I Remember Mama*, *I'll Walk Beside You*, *Rose of Tralee*, *Danny Boy*, *Wings of the Morning*, *Boys Town*, *Angels With Dirty Faces*, *Goodbye Mr Chips*, *Tom Brown's Schooldays*, *San Francisco*, *Rainbow on the River*, *State Fair*, *Music For Millions*, not

The Globe Cinema its lights dimmed shortly before demolition in the 1970s.

forgetting Roy Rogers and Dale Evans and *The March of Time*. Time marches on but we will not forget those magical movie memories provided by the Globe.

Mr B. Watson

An Everlasting Memorial

Portland Baths
Fairy princess jumping on the steps
For I was only a Meadows' kid
Into the wash-house
To wait for me mam
And then went home for me tea
Playing in the Rock Gardens
At Vic Embankment
Why it had that name
I just couldn't see
The Memorial Gardens
It shall be
I still reminisce
Of the life of yesterday
And my tomorrows
Thank you Meadows
It was a great place to be
Cheers for the memories
They can't take them away from me

Mrs Teresa Adcock

The Friendlier Society

My family lived at No. 55 Radcliffe Street, also my grandparents and auntie and uncle lived in Lamcote Street. One of my aunts had the corner shop there. I remember Mrs Smith, greengrocer, Mr Chester, newsagent, Mr Camms, chippy. Mam would send us to the tram sheds for a shilling's worth of pennies for the meters.

Dad was a driver for the LMS loco at Middle Furlong Road, the caller-up used to knock him up shouting at midnight 'one o'clock on'. A lot of railwaymen lived in the area including my grandad and uncle.

We went to St Gabriel's Sunday school and we often held an Anniversary day which included a gala parade in our new frocks. The Rock Gardens and the Rec' were our favourite haunts.

Most of the lads went to Meadows Boys' Club which is famous even today and some 'lads' still meet up. The late Peter Taylor, who enjoyed such glory days at Nottingham Forest with Brian Clough, was an old boy.

The Meadows was a good place to live, friendly and safe.

Brenda Lee Brown

CHAPTER 4

Celebrations

The Coronation party in 1953 at St Faith's Church Hall held for the children of Woolmer Road.

Monty Celebrated Victory

There was a chap who came into our class at London Road School and played the accordion. He came to celebrate VE Day at the school. We knew him as Monty. He did magic tricks as well. He was quite a character. I loved the Meadows. Everyone helped one another. You shared your joys and troubles and everyone cared.

Mary West (née Whitby)

Empire Day in the playground of London Road School, c. 1937. Pat Hanson is second from the left in the front row.

Tom Hart, father of Vera Stafford, celebrates the Queen's Coronation in 1953 in his backyard.

Above and below: *Parents and children of Crocus Street celebrate the end of the war in 1945.*

Above: *The Glapton Road children's party held in honour of the Coronation.* Below: *The adult helpers at the party. Mary Reed is second from the right in the back row and Mr Marriott, an unsung hero of the floods in 1947, is on the far left in the same row.*

Coronation celebrations, 1953. Above: decorations by Mrs Ivy Clarkstone-Priestley and her Bosworth Road neighbour. Below: a group outside the Clifton Miners' Welfare, with Nightingale's shop, on the corner of Bosworth Road and Hawthorne Street, in the background.

The Boys' Brigade leading members of the St John's Ambulance Brigade down the street on the Sunday after the Coronation. A sight and sound enjoyed by all, except those whose Saturday evening excesses required a more tranquil morning after!

The Trimmings Go Up

We really went to town for the Queen's Coronation in 1953. Me and my neighbour put out all the trimmings and decorated the windows and doors.

The Sunday morning after, the Boys' Brigade marched down Bosworth Road in front of the St John's Ambulance, which was often a feature on a Sunday morning, and how we loved it. You can see from the photographs the type of houses we lived in.

The house on the corner of Bosworth Road was where the midwife resided.

I. Clarkstone-Priestley (née Morley)

The Night of the PME

The Meadows had many churches and chapels, and these were all great centres of activity. There were groups for men, women and children, meeting every day somewhere. I used to laugh when my great-aunt used to say she was off to the 'PME', this was a 'Pleasant Monday Evening' at Queen's Drive chapel.

Anniversaries of the chapels were always big events, special preachers on the Sunday and special events on Monday evening. Sunday school Anniversary services were preceded by a parade through the streets (all the children wearing their best clothes and many carrying flowers), often led by a band.

A *Sunday school parade in 1954, pictured passing Heason's hardware shop on Kirkewhite Street. Freda Mulvey, then Haslam, who supplied the photograph, is carrying a coat and wearing a white ribbon in her hair. Note the cobble-stone street and policeman on bicycle.*

The pubs and the Co-op also had many community activities. On Saturday evening as you passed any pub, community singing would be in progress. Clubs and guilds would have community singing evenings often accompanied by a piano which even Mrs Mills would have declined to use.

Bridgeway Hall hosted many celebrity concerts. All the famous singers and musicians of the day came, Isobel Baillie, Hedle Nash, Robert Easters. I marvelled at the Serbian violinist Bratza, and also the comedian 'Stainless Stephen' (I believe there was no charge for entrance but a 'silver collection' was taken).

We didn't need the Albert Hall as all the best came down Arky. One singer, I remember, was a contralto called Clara Serena, she always wore a kind of tiara.

During the war, the hall's schoolroom became a British Restaurant, serving cheap, nourishing meals to help us eke out our rations.

I have some photos of the Queen's Coronation being celebrated by a children's party on Glapton Road. While many people will recognize councillor Roland Green, I would draw your attention to Mr Marriott. During the war, he was our air-raid warden, very hard-working and helpful but the night he was appreciated more than ever was in 1947. The Trent was rising and the houses in Glapton Road, particularly the south end where we lived, were threatened. He contacted all the householders, warning

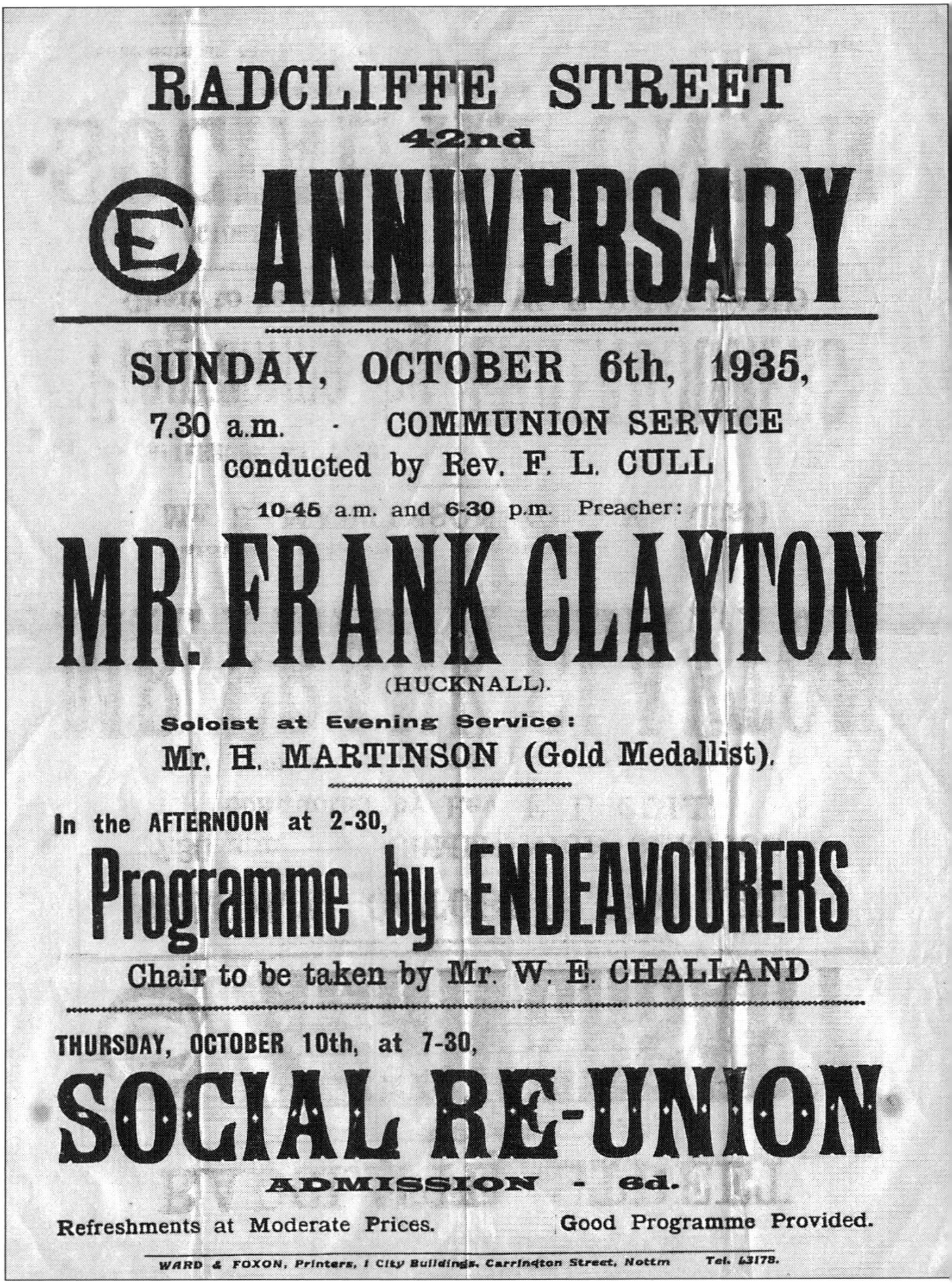

RADCLIFFE STREET
42nd
⊖ ANNIVERSARY

SUNDAY, OCTOBER 6th, 1935,

7.30 a.m. · COMMUNION SERVICE
conducted by Rev. F. L. CULL

10-45 a.m. and 6-30 p.m. Preacher:

MR. FRANK CLAYTON
(HUCKNALL).

Soloist at Evening Service:
Mr. H. MARTINSON (Gold Medallist).

In the AFTERNOON at 2-30,

Programme by ENDEAVOURERS

Chair to be taken by Mr. W. E. CHALLAND

THURSDAY, OCTOBER 10th, at 7-30,

SOCIAL RE-UNION
ADMISSION - 6d.

Refreshments at Moderate Prices.　　Good Programme Provided.

WARD & FOXON, Printers, 1 City Buildings, Carrington Street, Nottm　Tel. 63178.

Refreshments were promised at moderate prices as a poster lists some of the highlights and forthcoming attractions at the Radcliffe Street chapel as part of a Christian Endeavour Anniversary.

106

them and then set about helping those who needed it. My father was at work and we had a valuable piano. With the help of our next-door neighbour, he got the carpet up in the front room and then fetched firewood blocks from our coal-house and raised the piano to a safe height. My parents never forgot that kindness. Goodness knows how many other people he helped. This typified The Meadows' community spirit and he was most certainly one unsung hero from Glapton Road.

Another time of celebration was when the Duke of Edinburgh visited to open the flood prevention scheme and in true naval tradition, he came to The Meadows by boat along the River Trent.

Mary E. Reed (née Martison or to Mundellans 'Martoc')

Cattle Driven to Despair

From 1931 until 1938 together with my parents I lived in a seldom mentioned area called Melton Street, situated between Glebe Street and Kirkewhite Street. The only entrance and exit was from London Road. As well as Melton Terrace on the right-hand side of the street there was also a row of terraced houses on the left-hand side running across the end of the street. These were called Taylor's Cottages. Access was down an entry with each pair of houses sharing a backyard. Our house was one of the last two at the very end of the entry.

One day a herd of cattle being driven along London Road to the cattle market bolted off down Melton Street and ended up in our backyard. I was outside playing in the yard at the time as they came charging in.

The Duke of Edinburgh alights from his craft onto the north banks of the River Trent in 1949. The Great Central Railway bridge stands in the background. It was demolished in the 1970s shortly after the closure of Victoria Station.

A ladies' day out, embarking from the Clifton Hotel on Bosworth Road in 1940.

Luckily I ran back into the house as they entered. My mum was terrified of cows. I wasn't very keen on them myself after that episode. I well remember the look of relief on her face as I ran in through the back door, which she promptly locked. I'd be about four years old at the time.

Prior to my fifth birthday I started at London Road School. We celebrated Empire Day and my mother made dresses for the occasion, she being a dressmaker by trade. After a short period at the school my mother was told that I must take some time off as I was learning too quickly for my age. How times have changed!

There was a small shop on Melton Street where one could purchase a farthing's worth of sweets. After we left I was never able to buy a bag of sweets for that price again.

Every so often a street vendor would arrive pushing a handcart loaded with a huge block of salt. Many of the residents would purchase their salt from him.

When we first moved in we had an old black-leaded fireplace with an oven and boiler for hot water. Later my mother decided to replace it with something a little more up-to-date albeit still with an oven and boiler. There was no hot water system in any of the houses on the street at that time.

When the workmen removed the old fireplace both they and we were overrun with black clock beetles like cockroaches, that had been in residence at the back of the old grate. It took some time to exterminate them. There's no fun I can tell you getting up to a serving of dead beetles on the living-room floor every morning.

In 1938 we moved to a house with all mod cons. Hot water, bathroom etc!

One of my last memories of the old house was that of our old tin bath which we kept hanging on a wall in the yard when not in use. As we would have no further need for it, it was left for the incoming tenants.

Mrs Patricia M. Hanson

The swollen River Trent near Lovers' Walk tells its own story in 1947.

Date With Destiny Along Lovers' Walk

Throughout my life in The Meadows I never experienced a more dramatic moment than during the floods of 1947.

I was walking with my son Peter, aged four, and daughter Pam, just seven, across the suspension bridge to what was the Lovers' Walk side of the River Trent by the Becket School.

Planks of wood, doors and window frames were flowing like mad downstream. Suddenly, Peter lost his step and fell in. Pam was screaming and jumping up and down and twice I saw him go under and

where my husband Neville, who was working shifts on the buses, had no idea of the trauma we had been through.

I shall never forget the kindness of that lady or the floods of March 1947.

Peter is now a strapping big lad. As for my unborn son, he arrived in August of that year, when there was to be a royal wedding between Princess Elizabeth and Prince Philip. All the nurses wanted me to name him Philip, but I stuck with David. Truly a gift from God.

Eva Trueman

Eva on drier ground by the Embankment with Peter, Pam and little David safe and sound in the pram.

come back up. Eventually, after what seemed an eternity, I managed to pull Peter's head up above the water and get him back on the steps. It wasn't easy as I was expecting our third child at the time. Even so, the debris was threatening to sweep us both away but as I prayed to God, a tyre came floating that gave me enough support to undo the buttons on Peter's coat and untangle him from some floating rubbish.

By now onlookers had realized what was happening and came to drag us both to safety.

Having dried out at a lady's house nearby we got a taxi back to Kirkewhite Street

Pam, nineteen years of age, and David, pictured on the Embankment, near the scene of their mother's most dramatic escape eleven years previously.

The Damp Patches Come up for Air

My husband Roy Herbert (formerly Godber) lived in Derwent Street. His most vivid memory of The Meadows is the floods in 1947, when his family had their photo in the *Evening Post*. They were airing their furniture after the floods had subsided.

Mrs O.J. Herbert

Rising Damp

We lived at No. 9 Middle Furlong Road at the time of the floods of 1947. I recall the waters gradually rose over the weeks before drains and sewers burst everywhere. The water entered the house and left a trail of mud, sewage, etc., behind, including 6ft of water under the floor-boards.

E.A. Barnes

Shelter From the Storm

I have lived on Mundella Road since 1929 and have seen a lot of changes, more so where the new Meadows are now. I recall the floods of 1947 when the water ran amok on our street. During the Blitz of 8 and 9 May 1941, I vividly remember the bombing,

The water rising from the Trent engulfed many houses in The Meadows, including Mundella Road, pictured here on the morning of 11 March 1947.

Ex Nottingham Evening Post
June 7th, 1943

D.S.M. FOR NOTTM. MAN

"Outstanding Coolness And Courage"

Seaman-steward Dennis Cowli-shaw, whose home is at 47, Mundella-road, Nottingham, has been awarded the Distinguished Service Medal for bravery and skill during the passage of convoys to North Russia.

The official citation of the Admiralty states that he was recommended for "outstanding coolness and courage, rescuing survivors under heavy enemy fire

Seaman Cowlishaw.

with complete disregard of the splinters that were flying around; the occasion being that on which a convoy was attacked by three enemy destroyers and a Russian ship was sunk, and H.M.S. Lord Middleton proceeded between the opposing destroyers to rescue survivors. He has also shown fine qualities during the passage of two more convoys, and in the assistance shown to H.M.S. Somali, when she was torpedoed, and in the rescue work when she later sank under difficult weather conditions."

Seaman - steward Cowlishaw, who is 22 years of age, was employed by the Surgical Hosiery Co., Ltd., was educated at Trent Bridge School, and joined the Navy in 1940.

Left: *News of the citation in the local paper for Dennis Cowlishaw, DSM, who lived at No. 47 Mundella Road and attended Trent Bridge School. Another brother, Raymond, perished along with colleagues when the Co-op bakery, on the banks of the River Trent near Meadow Lane, sustained a direct hit during the night of the Nottingham Blitz of 8 May and the following morning of 9 May 1941. The Meadows was heavily bombed during this raid.*

when we used to shelter under the stairs, thinking it would give us some protection. When we emerged on the morning of 9 May I also witnessed the destruction of the whole lot of houses on Ryland Crescent and Bruce Grove.

Unfortunately, I lost a brother (Raymond) on the same night when the Co-op bakery on Meadow Lane was bombed.

Geoff Cowlishaw

[sadly Mr Cowlishaw passed away suddenly on 7 December 1999, aged seventy]

Bath Time in Deep Waters

Along with my late husband, Ivan, and our two daughters, Ann and Christine, we loved to take the steamer from Trent Bridge to Colwick Pleasure Beach just down the river. It was a marvellous day out for many Meadows folk.

My husband was born in King's Meadow Road and my mother-in-law lived two doors from the Mighty Atom's mother, now a 'Roly-Poly'. I'd see her visit sometimes.

My father-in-law was an engine-driver on Middle Furlong Road and mother-in-law worked for most of her life at the ROF factory at the top of her street.

I remember the floods of 1947 very well. My boyfriend, later my husband, decided to see me at the top end of Wilford Road to take me to meet his mother. However, the floods came almost to the Imperial Cinema so I could not go. There were boys in old tin baths wading through the water. Eventually we did most of our courting on the Embankment, on drier land! Yes we were poor but very happy. I could write more but arthritis in my fingers won't let me.

Betty Pearson (née Dickinson)

Residents on Hawthorne Street get their feet wet during March 1947. From left to right: Ida Hallam, Annie Edwards, Kathleen Edwards, Rosie Green, Frank Green and Dorothy Mulvey.

Betty Pearson, aged sixteen, pictured meeting her boyfriend at the Lions in the Old Market Square just after the Second World War.

When the Colonel's Statue was in Cold Water

I write with great trepidation hoping you will be able to read at least some of my writing, which I now find very difficult, due to being partially sighted.

My earliest recollection of life in The Meadows is being stood on the sink of No. 3 Launder Cottages to watch my sister Joan in the playground of Launder Street Church School. This would be about 1925 when I was two and my sister five years old. The school had closed as a weekday school before I was five, but continued as a Sunday school for St George's church for some time,

King's Meadow Road, home to the in-laws of Betty Pearson, March 1947.

and St George's Priory now stands on that site.

At No. 3 Launder Cottages and all other odd-numbered houses (ten in all) we had to share a lavatory between two houses until about 1930 when a further block of five were built.

On Monday 23 May 1932 my mother met my sister and I from school and we went to see the state of the river. My mother had been going to Wilford Bridge every hour, and by seven o' clock that evening, the water had risen to pass Colonel Clifton's statue. That was the signal to take everything possible upstairs, including a bath full of coal, newspapers and sticks, galvanized buckets of water and all the food in the house.

Next day was Empire Day, and we always had a half-day holiday from school. However, by morning, the streets and cellars were flooded and we wouldn't get to school at all. Fortunately, the water was not too high and only just lapped indoors when a vehicle came along. It had subsided by the next day. Later that year we moved across the road, to No. 10, which were bigger houses and each had a small garden, but still an outside loo and no bathroom.

After one term in the senior girls' school, I developed a bone disease, and spent almost a year in the General and Cedars hospitals, and this was the end of my school life at the age of eleven. As I was a wheelchair-user and there was no access for me I was not allowed to attend again, and was formally given a slip of paper at fourteen years old, informing me that my education was

Wilford Toll Bridge, almost engulfed by the Trent's swirling waters, March 1947.

completed! Fortunately, I had good parents and schoolteachers who did their utmost to help me acquire knowledge, and I was able to attend Cottesmore Evening Institute and Clarendon Institute for a good many evenings a week when I was able to walk again.

My father, Ernest Stedham, was a councillor for Meadows Ward 1933-1936 and 1945 until his death in 1951. He organized a train trip to Skegness on a Sunday in August for many years, threepence or sixpence a week being collected from early in the year. The train fare was 4s 6d, plus 6d for a bus from King's Meadow Road to the Victoria Station and back again at night. Everyone was guaranteed a seat (unusual on excursion trains) and 500 people went every year. For many it was their only outing of the year.

I have many memories of electioneering when children paraded the streets singing election songs and waving sticks with streamers attached. Happy days in The Meadows, so many memories.

Win Perkins (née Stedham)

Rising Tide and Soggy Cake

It was 19 March 1947. I was a fifteen-year-old apprentice hairdresser working at Rita's, No. 7 Wilford Road, overlooking the railway. We saw water coming along the railway lines about three o'clock. I received a phone call from home (we lived in Beeston Rylands at this time). 'Come home while you still can,' said my mother. Rita, who was a wonderful New Zealand lady, sent

Clifton Colliery, virtually marooned by the floods of 1947, viewed just upstream from the Toll Bridge.

me off to catch the train to Beeston. I remember the date so well as it was my little brother Keith's seventh birthday and Rita had made him a birthday cake from precious ingredients from a food parcel she'd received from back home in New Zealand, food still being seriously rationed.

Off I ran down Traffic Street when, whoops! I fell over and dropped the tin containing the precious cake. In a panic I scooped it up and ran on to catch the train. On arriving home flood water was coming up fast around the Rylands – the garden of our house already flooding. I found my mum and one of our lady neighbours, she had come to help with the party, chasing round the garden ankle-deep in water trying to round the chickens up so they wouldn't be drowned. Dad, in the meantime, was struggling and heaving with another

neighbour to get his precious piano on top of the dining-table, while half a dozen seven-year-olds were chasing round being 'birthday guests' of younger brother. As soon as they saw what I had brought home they were all clamouring around me for their slice of cake. Quickly retiring to the kitchen I tried my best to scrape the muddy bits of the cake with limited success – I told the kids that it was chocolate cake and the gritty bits were nuts – which they bravely tried to eat.

It was only many years later I confessed to Keith what really happened to his 'special birthday cake'. And as for dad's precious piano – it went through the floorboards rotted by the flood water – but that's another story!

Mrs Marj Bunfield (née Harris)

116

CHAPTER 6

Demolition

John Rowlson with daughter Maxine in 1977 standing on the spot where he once lived.

The end was nigh for The Meadows when officials of the city council's housing committee decided most of the region's accommodation was unfit for habitation. The final chapter about this unique community was about to be written. However, there are few words necessary to convey the demise of the neighbourhood. The pictures tell their own story...

Leaving the Meadows

I lived in Lamcote Street before moving to Glen Terrace, Rupert Street so that my mother Cis could be near my grandma Ada Rowlson in Moss Terrace. My father Jack was in the Army in North Africa. I left The Meadows in 1963 when I married.

John Rowlson

Before and after: London Road to the right of both pictures remains intact as does St Saviour's church, to the bottom left. To a far lesser degree, Arkwright Street, to the left, also stands. Little else survived once the Corporation had authorized the bulldozers to commence their slum clearance programme which obliterated communities not only in The Meadows but also the St Ann's district of the city during the early 1970s. (photographs: Nottingham Evening Post)

Burton's Almshouses on London Road in 1974, but their days, in keeping with much of the property thereabouts, were numbered. (photograph: Geoffrey Oldfield)

St Saviour's – Always on a Sunday

I was married at St Saviour's church in 1954 having been on St Saviour's Street and lived there. Although there was not much wealth about, we were rich beyond compare with friends and neighbours.

My sisters and I all went to St Saviour's Sunday school every Sunday. When it was over, our mum used to meet us and take us on a trip on the river to the Pleasure Park at Colwick and stay there until around seven o'clock; or we would just go for a walk along the Embankment, which was always busy with people; or through the Rock Gardens as we called them. A band often played in the bandstand, usually the Hames Hague Accordion Band.

We went to London Road School and we had to carry our gas masks with us as the war was on. After that we went to Trent Bridge School. Girls separate from the boys.

When you were eleven years old you could join the YWCA if you wished. It was on London Road, two houses knocked into one. You were taught various crafts plus natural movement dancing, we had some good times there.

There was never any shortage of friends to play with as most had big families. When my younger sister married they bought a house on Clayton Street off Queen's Drive. In 1969 they emigrated to Australia. They came back ten years later for a holiday and expected to knock on neighbours' doors and say hello again, but they couldn't believe everything and everybody had gone. As she said the heart had been ripped out of a community.

Arkwright Street was a hive of activity, you could get everything that was needed there, no need to go to town. We bought all our furniture, lino, rugs, etc., when we were setting up home from Cash Road at the corner of Ryehill Street. Oh happy, happy days.

June Clubbe (née Reesby)

Queen's Drive, once the epitome of Victorian elegance with its tree-lined vista, was reduced to this, one of the last houses to go in July 1976. (photograph: H.L. Mercer)

The vibrancy and congestion of Traffic Street had disappeared, pictured from Wilford Road. (photograph: H.L. Mercer)

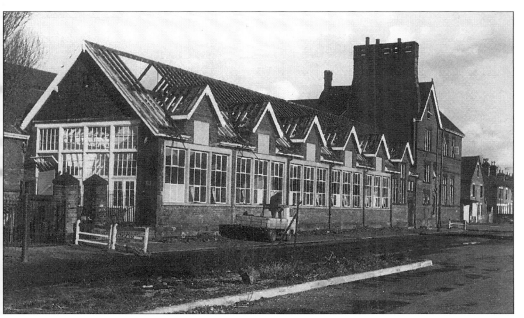

Bosworth Road School: through its doors thousands of Meadows children progressed from an idyllic childhood. The bell had long since tolled for its classes in 1975. (photograph: Michael Gardner)

Left: *Residents of Rutland Terrace off Bunbury Street in August 1969 – the writing was on the wall for most Meadows folk by then.* Below: *East Midlands Gas Board workers near Bunbury Street go about their work during the flattening process. (photographs: Geoffrey Oldfield)*

Miss Alice Harby, organist of St Saviour's church who lived on the Victoria Embankment, photographed by Geoffrey Oldfield. Alice Harby herself captured many of the faces and places during the last days of The Meadows.

A pair of trousers hanging out to dry in the back alleys of Briar Street appear to gesture an inverted final sign of defiance to authority in 1975. (photograph: Michael Gardner)

CHAPTER 7

Meadows of Joy

Joy Robinson-Judd aged fourteen and her sister Pauline aged one both lived at No. 77 Midland Crescent. In later life Joy wrote about her childhood in The Meadows in her autobiography Journey Back in Time, *as well as in the pages of* Bygones, *a publication of the* Nottingham Evening Post. *The following extracts are taken from her book.*

If ever the epithet 'Meadows born and bred' was apposite to anyone it is Joy Robinson-Judd, pictured right in 1947 in her Women's Junior Air Corps uniform. She has produced her own chronicles and memoirs, in essays and verse, that recall a quite unique way of life. As well as providing a charming insight and invaluable social document, some of these illuminating extracts from her texts and personal photographs paint an evocative picture of the way they were in The Meadows.

House Proud Neighbours

The Meadows – sounds romantic doesn't it, but it was in fact rows upon rows of streets with tightly packed houses consisting of two-up and two-down as the inhabitants called them.

Most of the houses were occupied by railwaymen and their families or miners, as The Meadows was near to the coal-pits and the railway. The houses were built so close together it was almost possible to lean out of the bedroom window and shake hands with your next-door neighbour. It was a constant source of amusement to see everyone trying to outdo his or her neighbour with different curtains or a prize potted plant in the window.

All the doorsteps were made of stone and every weekend they were scrubbed well and a white or yellow stone colour was applied, and woe betide putting a dirty shoe mark on the step until it had dried.

The houses were very Victorian and consisted of parlour, kitchen and scullery. The parlour was the first room entered by the front door straight off the street – this was a through room and the stairs were between this room and the kitchen, which was not a kitchen as we know them today, but a living-room with a huge black cast-iron fire-grate dominating the room. The scullery was a small kitchen with a brownstone sink about 4 inches deep and set so low down one had to bend to wash up in it. The tap – only a cold water tap – was so high up above this sink that it splashed everyone who used it, and every time the tap was turned on it rattled and banged. The pipes to this tap were made of lead and when a pipe sprung a leak the plumber repaired it and it looked like a huge metal blister or bulge, I understand this was called a wiped joint. The large black fire-grate in the kitchen had to be cleaned weekly with a special black liquid polish called Zebo. It had a high fire-grate basket – almost knee-high – and a highly polished brass or copper type hood sloping up into the chimney space. There was a large oven on the right and a water container on the left. When these grates had had the weekly clean they glowed beautifully in the firelight and shone like black and grey gunmetal.

Fantasy Islands

Childhood was full of fantasy for us in The Meadows, we used to borrow a pair of Mum's high-heeled shoes, usually four sizes too big, and paddle round the yard pretending we were kings and queens or movie stars. The old velvet table-cloth was a magnificent cloak, that is until we got caught with it.

I remember one particular New Year's Day when I was about seven and my brother aged nine and I were playing in the snow, which had fallen heavily that night, and we were building an igloo in the corner of the fence. This task took us all day and we could see Mother inside the house preparing the table for tea and when she called us in and gave us hot buttered crumpets, or 'pikelets' as they called them, they were absolutely delicious. This incident remains in my memory, for never again will crumpets taste quite as nice as they did that day. After being put out in the cold all day our faces glowed bright red like the coal fire – almost a perfect start to a brand new year.

Honey – and Gran – Knew Best

Our paternal grandmother had many talents and could set her hand to almost anything. She could make clothes out of the smallest pieces of cloth and laboriously unpicked garments to make us newish outfits. She helped at babies' births and even laid people out. She had her own pet remedies for illness and cured many a youngster's whooping cough with her own remedy, which consisted of a jar of white vinegar and a new-laid egg – uncooked – which she put in the vinegar and left for seven days and nights. The egg was put into the jar complete in its shell and after a few days it started to disintegrate. After seven days the egg had completely gone and Gran gave the liquid a good whisk and added a tablespoonful of honey and a squeeze of lemon juice. This liquid was then administered to any child with whooping cough and it always seemed to work.

Scrumping – Then a Wallop

We used to go scrumping then. If we knew of a house or garden that had apple trees we would scale the very highest walls. If we got caught by the local policeman he would always say: 'Do you want me to wallop you or shall I take you to your dad?' We always preferred a gentle wallop from the policeman and it never seemed to do us any lasting harm.

Grandma Clarke in the yard of the Castle Inn on Wilford Road.

A Superstitious Lot

Whenever a new baby arrived everyone wanted to call in and see it, but some wouldn't go over the doorstep until the new mother had been 'churched' for they claimed it to be unlucky.

They were a superstitious lot. No one would wash their clothes on New Year's Day, not even a pocket-handkerchief. For it was said that anyone who washed clothes on New Year's Day would wash a loved one away. Newly-weds sometimes pooh-poohed this superstition, but invariably during the next twelve months some member of the family died and they were greeted with 'I told you so.' Even if the member of the family was someone's uncle twice removed who died, it was always put down to this superstition.

I think I was practically brought up on superstitions. Do not walk under ladders, do not cross knives on the table. Do not put new shoes on a table. Do not brush the table with a broom.

We were quoted 'Brush the table with broom, brush a coffin in the room.' If a bird fell down the chimney it was regarded as a bad omen.

People in The Meadows would never wash blankets in the month of May for that too was regarded as washing away one's loved ones.

May blossom was absolutely taboo. No child could bring May blossom into the house without incurring the wrath of the household.

Four-leaf clovers were swooped on and gently pressed in a flower press for luck, and horseshoes were prized. An old lady I visited once gave me some peacock feathers and I was forbidden to bring them into the house as they were regarded as very unlucky.

Last Orders, Ladies and Gentlemen, Please

There seemed to be a lot of public houses in The Meadows and two I recall along Wilford Road were the Castle and the Locomotive Inn. The latter was so named because it was quite near to the railway shunting yard. Nearly all the railwaymen spent their social hours in this pub. Saturday was the most popular night to visit the local pub and there was always singing and lots of noise coming from the open windows.

The furniture in the houses down The Meadows was mostly of the comfortable type. Usually there was a sofa and a big kitchen table, which normally had a white polished top and could be scrubbed clean if necessary. Sometimes there was an assortment of dining-chairs. The rugs by the fire were usually home-made and the floor was covered in shiny linoleum. Not many homes had a vacuum cleaner in those days and the house had to be swept out every day in order to keep it clean. Gran had a lovely big brass fender in the parlour around the fireplace and a little trivet shaped like a miniature brass table with a copper kettle standing proudly on it. These brass and copper articles were polished daily. On the doors were lovely copper finger-plates depicting grapes and vines and these too received a daily polish. They were absolutely beautiful – wonder what happened to them? Everything seemed to be geared to warmth and cosiness and we never seemed cold in those days even though there was no central heating.

Gone are these houses now, and in their place stand modern homes with all amenities and facilities one expects in a home of today. It is also very difficult to find now. The 'old Meadows' may not be around now but for people like myself the memories linger on.

Printed in Great Britain
by Amazon